COLD WAR

THE AMERICAN CRUSADE
AGAINST WORLD COMMUNISM
1945–1991

COLD WAR

THE AMERICAN CRUSADE
AGAINST WORLD COMMUNISM
1945–1991

JAMES A. WARREN

LOTHROP, LEE & SHEPARD BOOKS

NEW YORK

FIRST EDITION

10 9 8 7 6 5 4 3

Library of Congress Cataloging in Publication Data

Warren, James A.
Cold War: the American crusade against world
communism, 1945-1991 / James A. Warren.
p.   cm.
Includes bibliographical references (p.263).
ISBN 0-688-10596-3
1. United States—Foreign relations—Soviet Union—Juvenile literature.
2. Soviet Union—Foreign relations—United States—Juvenile literature.
3. United States—Foreign relations—1945-1989—Juvenile literature.
4. Cold War—Juvenile literature. 5. World politics—1945- —Juvenile literature. I. Title.
E183.8.S65W375 1995 327.73047—dc20   94-24554 CIP AC

In memory of
JAMES D. WARREN
Uncle, soldier, teacher, friend

ACKNOWLEDGMENTS

Special thanks to my editor, Ruth I. Gordon, Ph.D. who insisted that every word count. Ruth's thoughtful, probing questions and insights improved this account of America's longest war more than I can say. Thanks to David Warren, professor of political science at the University of Rhode Island, and Judit Bodnar for reading the manuscript and offering many helpful suggestions. Richard Gallin did a superb job of copyediting *Cold War*, for which I am most grateful. Susan Pearson at Lothrop believed in the project from start to finish, and Melanie Donovan saw the project through completion with grace and good humor. Finally, thanks to Grace Warren and Paul Warren for unstinting moral support.

CONTENTS

Several months before leaving office, President George Washington published in 1796 a memorable address to the American people in which he outlined his "great rule of conduct" concerning the foreign affairs of the United States of America. Insofar as it was possible, wrote the first president, the nation should "steer clear of permanent Alliances," and only in extraordinary emergencies should foreign alliances be formed at all.

The "Farewell Address" is one of the most enduring and influential expressions of what historians call American isolationism: the idea that the United States should focus its energies on domestic matters and leave the rest of the world pretty much to its own devices. Broadly speaking, the United States Government followed the advice of its first president until 1941, when the Japanese attack on the U.S. fleet at the Pearl Harbor naval base in Hawaii drew the country into a global conflict from which it emerged in 1945 as the most powerful nation, economically and militarily, in world history.

Great power often goes hand in hand with great responsibility. This was certainly true in the case of the United States in 1945, for on its shoulders fell a heavy burden. A devastated Europe had to be rebuilt. A new system of world trade was needed. Even before World War II had ended, plans were carried forward to fashion a global collective security system, a way for nations to join together to protect themselves and to act together against any attacking nation. Perhaps most urgently—at least from the viewpoint of the American political leaders of the time—a strategy had to be developed and implemented to confront the spread of world communism. The great concern was that the "Red menace" would spread from the Union of Soviet Socialist Republics (which was often called the Soviet Union or simply the USSR) across all Europe, thereby "enslaving" precisely those peoples who had just been liberated from Nazi Germany. It was widely believed that world communism posed a serious threat to what Westerners of the era called "Christian civilization."

Containing communism within the borders of the Soviet Union would not be easy. The Soviet Union had a very large, battle-hardened army and a leader who was highly skilled, ruthless, and committed to the revolutionary ideals of Marxist-Leninism, which linked human progress with the destruction of Western democracy and capitalism. Communism offered a penetrating and alluring critique of the problems and inequities of the modern democracies; it held immense appeal for the downtrodden peoples of the world, of whom (thanks to the great destruction of World War II) there were a great many.

The American struggle against communism lasted for almost fifty years. This book is an introductory history of that conflict. It aims to acquaint the reader with the major policies and crises of the worldwide conflict widely known as the cold war. In addition to describing the key events, forces, and themes that made the cold war what it was, I have tried to bring to life the thinking and the emotions of the key decision makers. For it is only in coming to know the worldview of the key players that the full meaning and drama of the cold war emerge.

The cold war was above all else complex. It was at one and the same time a military, diplomatic, economic, and scientific rivalry. It was also a struggle between two very powerful ideas. Although the United States and the Soviet Union were the leading powers, they were by no means the only ones. The rivalry played itself out all over the world. Hundreds of thousands died fighting for one side or the other in places such as Korea, Ethiopia, Nicaragua, Malaya, and Vietnam. Cold war issues figured prominently in most of the crises that beset the international community during the last half century.

In short, the struggle between East and West had implications for everyone on the planet. People everywhere seemed to grasp that there was something unique about this great-power rivalry. It wasn't just that these two nations supported the largest armed forces in human history; there was something qualitatively different. As

Thomas Larson wisely observed in his book *Soviet-American Rivalry,* "The vulnerability to weapons that could destroy entire countries . . . heightened fears and antagonisms and made the struggle for power and influence appear to be also a struggle for survival."

In the early stages of the research for this project, I realized that some difficult choices had to be made about the scope of the book. A comprehensive history of the confrontation, exploring every point of view at the same level of detail, would have taken several volumes, as well as knowledge of a number of languages with which I have no familiarity. So I decided to focus my research and writing on the still large, but far more manageable, topic of the American crusade against the Soviet Union that involved the political ideas and ideals on which those nations were founded. Anticommunism, aside from being the great theme of recent U.S. foreign policy, was an abiding preoccupation of the people of the United States for half a century. It made an enduring mark on our institutions, our view of the world, even our sense of what it means to be an American.

To bring that subject to life, I decided to explore the attitudes and policies of the leaders of many nations, especially those of the Soviet Union and it allies. I also attempted to put the key issues and crises of the East-West conflict into a global context so that readers would be able to see the broad significance of the events and policies I was describing.

A brief word now about bias and objectivity in writing history and, more particularly, in writing this book.

Historians are supposed to be dispassionate, objective observers of the past—not partisan commentators or pleaders for a cause. In the case of a survey history of an American crusade written by an American, this is a tall order, and one that, I confess, I cannot wholly fill. Since my own political beliefs have at the very least shaped the set of questions I've examined in this book, it seems only fair to let the reader know something about them.

I am basically sympathetic to the major objectives of the United States in waging the cold war. I felt at the outset of writing this book that, as the American theologian Reinhold Niebuhr once put it, "Man's inclination to justice makes democracy possible, but man's inclination to injustice makes democracy necessary." I still feel that way. The collapse of the Soviet Communist system, within the Soviet Union itself as well as in Eastern Europe, lends credence to this aphorism.

The United States is, of course, very far from a perfect democracy, but during the cold war years it was the leading proponent of basic democratic principles and institutions. The country's foreign-policy leaders pursued courses of action that were first and foremost in the national interest of the United States, and that is as it should be. But that did not mean that those policies were inherently self-serving, for underlying the policies and ideas of the Americans there was always a profound sense of moral responsibility. The United States, as leader of the West, was obliged to use its resources and energies to expand the boundaries of the democratic world. Communism was inherently antidemocratic. It had to be challenged, and it was.

Many of the historians who have been highly critical of U.S. foreign policies during the cold war era, and who see those policies largely as a smoke screen for American empire building, appear to have lost sight of how firmly this notion of moral responsibility was fixed in the minds of American decision makers from the 1920s through the 1980s.

Good intentions, however, do not always lead to good policy. The United States, in the course of fighting its crusade against world communism, made mistakes, misjudgments, and moral compromises. Even the most ardent supporter of that era's U.S. foreign policy must recognize that many of the initiatives designed to combat communism may have done little but strengthen its hold. This, it seems to me, was what transpired in Vietnam, where much of what the Americans did was based on the arrogant belief that what was good for the United States was by definition good for the Vietnamese. And Vietnam was by no means the only case in which the moralistic zeal of the Americans came to a bad end.

What was the cause of this great conflict, and why did it last so long? I don't believe there is a simple answer to either of these questions. No single event, no one force, brought the cold war into being. True enough, the peoples of the United States and of the Soviet Union had vastly different traditions and histories. Their governments had divergent interests and faced different problems. But this alone doesn't explain the peculiar hostility and bitter competition that characterized their relationship between 1945 and 1990.

Circumstances beyond the direct control of either

government, in my view, played a large role. The defeat of Hitler's Germany left uncertainty and a power vacuum of great magnitude in Europe. Who would control the vast resources of Germany, the continent's industrial heartland? The German government had for all intents and purposes ceased to exist. A vanquished Germany meant that the United States and the Soviet Union were bound to butt heads, even while they attempted, immediately after the war, to work together to shape a new world. The struggle of both governments to fill that vacuum was marked by misunderstanding, mistrust, and disillusionment, all of which did much to cement hostile attitudes. Those attitudes, once formed, proved remarkably durable.

Perhaps it is true, as some have argued, that no matter how determined some diplomats and politicians in Washington and Moscow were to escape a distorted, overly negative view of their adversary, the relationship would have been rocky at best. Communism and democratic capitalism, after all, offer fundamentally different views of history, government, economics, and morality. The democratic capitalist's view of the role of the individual, and of his or her rights and responsibilities to society, is at complete odds with the view of the Communist. Indeed, the two parties to this rivalry had almost nothing in common upon which to build a constructive relationship. This being the case, it seems unlikely that any sort of harmonious relationship would have emerged, even under less trying circumstances.

In the course of writing the book, I found that my attitude toward the key decision makers (with a few exceptions), both Soviet and American, was increasingly one of respect for their sense of commitment, their unflagging dedication, and their willingness to sacrifice for causes in which they deeply believed. And I came to admire the restraint and discipline on both sides. The cold war could very easily have ended in nuclear holocaust.

Thoughtful people from both East and West regularly warned that nuclear war was a live option. But as we now know, there was to be no such conflagration. Much of the credit for this lies with the statesmen, soldiers, and diplomats who worked on the front lines of the cold war.

The cold war was fought by many people, over a long period of time, on a variety of battlefields. The more I studied this vast subject, the more convinced I became that great truths and grand statements about the conflict are almost always suspect. Reasonable people can disagree on most of the important questions concerning the long history of the cold war, and they often do. If you hear or read of a sweeping condemnation of the United States' policy in Latin America, or the Soviet Union's in Eastern Europe, my advice is to take a look for yourself. You will probably find that the truth is more elusive. In writing this book, I felt it was important to keep that idea in mind. I believed it was essential, above all else, to understand the participants on their terms, to see the world, its opportunities and threats, through their eyes. Where I have made judgments and assessments of actions and policies—and inevitably one has to do so in a survey history of this sort—I tried to do so with fairness and restraint.

CHAPTER ONE

THE END . . .
AND THE BEGINNING

On November 9, 1989, a curious and unexpected event occurred: Hundreds of people danced merrily atop a long and forbidding wall that divided the German city of Berlin into eastern and western sectors. In the ensuing days, thousands more Germans joined the party, taking up shovels, picks, anything they could find, and setting about the happy task of breaking this barrier, the Berlin Wall, apart.

That the Germans undertook this task of destruction in a spirit of celebration was hardly surprising. The Berlin Wall had been constructed in the summer of 1961 by the order of the premier of the Soviet Union, Nikita Khrushchev. Designed to cut off the flow of East German citizens into the Western sector of the city, it was soon transformed into something more than just another state-imposed barrier, another grim reminder that the arm of government was everywhere in Eastern Europe. It became the most prominent symbol of the tension and rivalry between democratic capitalism and communism, between the West (the United States, Britain, France, and their allies), and the East (the Soviet Union, the nations of Eastern Europe, and their allies).

The rivalry had been, without question, the most expensive, the most global, and certainly the most dangerous of any in recorded history. Two nations of enormous strength, the Union of Soviet Socialist Republics in the East and the United States of America in the West, had played the leading roles, but the Germans themselves had played a major part. For it was in Germany, and over Germany, that the cold war began. And in Germany, in November of 1989, the cold war was surely coming to an end.

Many of the Germans in Berlin that November had spent their entire lives in a divided Germany, but many other Berliners still remembered the beginning of the cold war more than four decades earlier. The fall of the wall, insofar as it presaged the fall of communism in East Germany and in the rest of Eastern Europe, was a decidedly welcome development—all the more so because communism seemed about to leave the world stage, in Germany at least, not with a bang but with a whimper. Over the next two years, the nations that had fallen under the control of the powerful Soviet army in Eastern Europe in the final days of World War II would reject their established governments; for better or worse, they would opt for revolution, for self-determination, for a future dictated by their own choices.

What made all of this possible? Although the roots of

unrest and dissatisfaction with the status quo in Eastern Europe were deep, it took the policies of one forward-looking leader of the Soviet Union, Mikhail Gorbachev, to make true reform and revolution a live option. Gorbachev's policies of *glasnost* (roughly translated as "openness") and *perestroika* ("restructuring") turned out to be far more explosive than he or any other Communist bargained for. In December 1991, after a series of secessions and attempted secessions by the USSR's member republics, and even a last-gasp coup by hard-liners, the famous red flag with hammer and sickle came down from the Kremlin. The world's most powerful Communist state ceased to exist, its fifteen republics all claiming some new form of independence. The great and fearsome Soviet empire was defunct.

The fall of the USSR signaled many things, but most of all it meant that the cold war era had come to an abrupt and unforeseen end. The cold war spanned more than four decades. It was a time, historian Bernard Weisberger tells us, "of denunciations, propaganda, coups, proxy wars, invasions, alliances, and arms buildups, punctuated by brief episodes of cooperation, but always veering perilously toward the brink of nuclear holocaust."[1] In the end, the cold war was a conflict between two vastly different systems and the people who believed in them. It was a peculiar and complex conflict, fought on more levels than other wars in modern history. And for those who participated, the stakes were indeed high: The very survival of the planet hung in the balance.

* * *

Our story begins in April 1945, when two great armies converged on the Elbe River in Germany: the Soviet Union's Red Army from the east and the United States Army from the west. When they met at the Elbe, there was much rejoicing, for the Third Reich (Adolf Hitler's Germany) was in its death throes. The surrender of the Germans to the Allies in May created a power vacuum of monumental proportions in Europe, and it set the stage for the coming confrontation between the Soviet Union and the United States.

The seeds of conflict between the two nations, however, predated World War II and Germany's subsequent surrender. The Americans and the Western Europeans shared a political and social culture based on the ideas of the ancient Greeks, the Enlightenment, and British common law. An abiding respect for individual rights, private property, representative government, the rule of law, and a free press was at its core.

The Bolsheviks, a group of inspired revolutionaries, had seized power late in 1917 from a provisional government that had overthrown the Russian czar earlier that year. The Bolsheviks scorned the political traditions and institutions of the West. At first the revolutionaries ruled Russia by assemblies called soviets. Soon soviet republics were also set up in Ukraine, Belarus, and other parts of what had been the czarist Russian empire. Drawing on the outlook and philosophy of the nineteenth-century German philosopher Karl Marx, they created a Communist system committed to the overthrow of democratic governments, which they considered not democratic at all. To Vladimir Ilych Lenin, the charismatic leader of the Communist movement, democracies seemed little more than governments designed to enhance the lives of the factory owners and landed aristocrats at the expense of the working class (Marx had referred to working people as the proletariat).

It was Lenin's belief that over time the capitalist democracies would reach a crisis point. This crisis in the capitalist states, Lenin and other Marxists reasoned, would inevitably lead to a "dictatorship of the proletariat." The oppressed workers would rise up against their exploiters to create a society without the profound inequities and injustices that afflicted Western societies and had afflicted czarist Russia. After the workers had gained power, the great inequities and injustices endemic to capitalist government and institutions would disappear, to be replaced with a kind of heaven on earth, a workers' utopia where no government at all would be necessary.

The new Communist government in Russia abolished private property, seized the factories and banks, confiscated everyone's bank accounts, and ordered that land be distributed to the peasants. The Communists also abolished Russia's old court and police systems. They refused to repay the debts of the old czarist government or compensate people for seized property—actions that shocked and enraged foreign investors.

These Communist ideas and actions worried people in the Western countries. They were understandably nervous about Communist intentions. Did the Russian Communists intend to carry revolution throughout Europe? How, people in the West asked themselves, could this newly established government join the community of nations if its stated objective was to subvert the governments of those nations? These were tough questions. It was more than a matter of Communist Russian intentions. There was a disturbing fanaticism that Americans as well as Europeans detected in the Marxist outlook. Lenin, musing on the inevitability of conflict between the two world views, had once written that there was "no other alternative. Either the Soviet government triumphs in every advanced country in the world, or the most reactionary imperialism triumphs, the most savage imperialism which is throttling the small and feeble nationalities and reinstating reaction all over the world." [2]

These sentiments were by no means uncommon among Communist leaders and spokesmen in the years following the Bolshevik Revolution of 1917. They engendered a good deal of fear and wrath in the United States. Yet a small but ardent group of American Communists, headquartered in big cities such as New York and Chicago, carried the movement's message forward. Their proselytizing stirred a deep distrust, sometimes bordering on hysteria, of Communists and their ideas. Woodrow Wilson, the U.S. president at the time of the 1917 revolution, spoke for many Americans in saying that Bolshevism was immoral and even unnatural.

Americans were troubled, too, by the contradictions of communism. The Communists disdained organized religion—it was the "opiate of the people"—but the doctrine of communism itself seemed to bear many of the characteristics of a religion. Furthermore, Lenin and his

disciples talked a great deal about equality and brotherhood, but in practice, Bolshevism placed extraordinary
power in the hands of a self-appointed elite. The leaders
of the Bolshevik Revolution *claimed* to speak for the
people, but in fact they displayed little or no interest in
the people's opinions. Freedom of speech and freedom
of the press were ignored. Many of those who spoke out
in dissent in the fledgling Soviet state were simply taken
out and shot.

Far from bringing progress and prosperity to the
Russian people, the new leaders of the Soviet Union
were doing all they could to secure a monopoly of economic and political power—or so it seemed to most
observers. While some in the United States, disturbed by
the moral and economic injustices of capitalism, found
Marx's ideas refreshing (the journalist John Reed was
perhaps the most famous example), the vast majority of
people in the United States were appalled by the
Communists' utter disregard for freedom as Americans
understood it and by their ruthlessness in pursuing their
objectives. Could communism spread, like some
hideous virus, to the shore of the American Republic?
Just a few years after the outbreak of the Russian
Revolution, many thought it already had. Fears were
magnified by Marx's belief that Communist revolution
would most likely take hold not in an agrarian culture
such as Russia, but in highly industrialized societies,
where the injustices suffered by the working class were
most pronounced.

It was out of this climate of fear and mistrust that the
first Red Scare in U.S. history emerged in the last years

of World War I and reached its peak in late 1919 and early 1920. So deep was the fear of communism in the United States that people were sometimes jailed for simply voicing Communist or Socialist ideas. Eugene V. Debs, who had been a Socialist Party candidate for the U.S. presidency in 1900, 1904, 1908, and 1912, was put in prison in 1918 for advocating "subversive" ideas. Foreigners were routinely detained or arrested for no other reason than that they might be harboring leftist political notions. In 1919, the U.S. Government began to deport hundreds of radical aliens. By early 1920, Attorney General A. Mitchell Palmer had ordered a series of raids across the United States during which police arrested several thousand suspected radicals.

Politicians exploited the fears of ordinary Americans, calling upon them to resist the evil forces of revolution. "Like a prairie fire," wrote Attorney General Palmer,

> the blaze of revolution was sweeping over every American institution of law and order. . . . It was eating its way into the homes of the American workman, its sharp tongues of revolutionary heat were licking the altars of the churches, leaping into the belfry of the school bell, crawling into the sacred corners of American homes, seeking to replace marriage vows with libertine laws, burning up the foundations of society. [3]

In 1922, after several years of civil war, Communist-controlled Russia, Belarus, Ukraine, and other regions officially united to become the Union of Soviet Socialist Republics. Within a year after Lenin's death in 1924, Britain, Italy, France, and other countries gave diplomatic recognition to the Soviet Union. Nevertheless, the United States refused to recognize the Communist dictatorship until 1933. Lenin's successor, Joseph Stalin (born in Georgia, which had been part of the old Russian empire and which had become part of the Soviet Union in 1922), did much to establish his absolute power. He had a shrewd grasp of politics and was determined to make the Soviet Union into a major player on the world stage—at any price.

The key to achieving this status lay, of course, in building up the Soviet economy and in modernizing the army. Stalin, who possessed more than his share of the ancient Russian penchant for security and secrecy, put his country on a permanent war footing. Tanks and guns took precedence over food, housing, and consumer goods in his efforts to change the nation from a preindustrial society to a modern country able to compete with, and eventually overthrow, other nations.

The Soviet leader's quest to build his nation's industrial might in the 1920s and 1930s was successful, but it came at a great cost to the peoples of the Soviet Union, who had to endure tremendous hardships so their dictator's dreams might be realized. Stalin, who Winston Churchill (among other Western leaders) felt had "genuine charm," had no concern for human life if it stood in the way of his own ambitions. Indeed, Adolf Hitler was his only rival when it came to terror and mass murder. Historians believe that in his quest to solidify his power after Lenin's death, Stalin may have been responsible for the deaths of as many as twelve million people. Millions of ordinary people with no political beliefs whatsoever died of starvation and overwork, especially when Stalin forced them to give up their private farms and join huge state-run collective farms. Whole groups of potential rivals, including millions of Communist Party members, disappeared in the infamous purges of the 1930s. Little wonder, then, that relations between Russia and the powers of the West were as cold as ice.

While Stalin was busy transforming backward Russia into a modern, industrialized state, Adolf Hitler was preparing a powerful military machine in Germany. By the late 1930s there were storm clouds over all Europe. Many statesmen felt that Hitler had designs on the whole of Europe, perhaps the entire world. Hitler knew that, at least initially, he couldn't fight Britain and France in the west and Stalin's Soviet Union in the east at the same time. So he negotiated a nonaggression pact with Stalin. The agreement, signed and announced to the world in August 1939, included the promise that Nazi Germany and the Soviet Union would not attack each other. If either were attacked by a third nation, the other signer would remain neutral. There was, however, a secret part of the pact: Poland was to be invaded and divided between Germany and the Soviet Union. Nevertheless, Stalin feared it was only a matter of time until the German dictator turned his eyes (and his army) eastward, but the pact gave the Soviet Union precious time to prepare for that possibility.

Eight days after the pact between the Soviet Union

and Germany was sealed, Germany invaded Poland, and World War II began. The Axis powers (Germany, Italy, and Japan) waged war against the Allied powers. In June 1941, after Hitler had taken a huge chunk of western European territory (including France, the Netherlands, Denmark, Belgium, and Norway), the Wehrmacht (Germany's army) turned eastward and invaded Russia. At this point the United States, although technically neutral, was already giving large amounts of matériel and aid to Britain and its allies. Four days after Germany's ally Japan attacked the United States naval base at Pearl Harbor on December 7, 1941, Germany declared war on the United States. Now the United States joined Britain and the Soviet Union in their commitment to destroy Hitler and the expanding Nazi empire.

From 1941 to 1945 the "Big Three"—the United States, the Soviet Union, and Great Britain—fought the Nazi menace bravely; none more so than the Russians, whose casualties were far more severe than those of any other combatant nation. Given the widely divergent political ideas and the recent friction between East and West, the alliance held together well. One of the reasons for the goodwill between the Soviet Union and the United States was that President Franklin D. Roosevelt had mounted a crusade to alter America's negative impression of all things Soviet. The dreaded Communist menace was almost overnight transformed by a gigantic U.S. propaganda machine into a trustworthy ally, one that supposedly shared the same vision of a postwar democratic world as our longtime allies, Britain and France.

But the war against Hitler and the close alliance with the Western powers didn't change Stalin's beliefs or attitudes. He remained a devoted Communist, which meant he stood against the institutions and values of the West. He remained a glutton for personal power. The Soviet premier's handling of matters in Eastern Europe (where the Red Army reigned supreme in 1945 and afterward) proved this. Despite his having signed a series of agreements concerning the conquered territories and the importance of establishing governments based on self-determination and democracy, the Soviet Union had no intention of allowing these countries—Czechoslovakia, Romania, Poland, Bulgaria, and Hungary among them—to shape their own destinies.

It was not immediately clear that Stalin would take this position. As the cement that held the alliance together—the threat of a Nazi-controlled Europe—began to fall away, so did the harmony among the Allies. Mutual fear and suspicion began to creep in. There was Stalin's not-unfounded fear of collusion between the British and the Americans; they spoke the same language, after all, and together they had resisted the Soviet dictator's pleas to attack Germany from the west in 1942 or 1943. When the Western Allies' armies did invade the shores of German-occupied France on June 6, 1944, Stalin observed that it was about time the British and the Americans began to help reduce "the enormous sacrifices of the Soviet armies, compared with which the sacrifices of the Anglo-American armies are insignificant."[4] Throughout the war, Stalin, Roosevelt, and Churchill, the leaders of the Big Three Allies, were very much aware of the magnitude of change that defeat of the Axis powers would bring to the world. They had discussed, almost continually, the shape of the new order that would emerge once Germany and Japan had been crushed. One of the most important of the conferences held during the war years took place at Yalta, a resort town in the Soviet Crimea, in February 1945. At that point the Russians were in a strong bargaining position regarding the fate of the nations of Eastern Europe, as their army had already made deep inroads there.

The U.S. delegation at Yalta, led by an ailing President Franklin D. Roosevelt, was anxious to have Stalin (also in attendance) commit Soviet forces to the fight against Japan. This the Soviets agreed to do in exchange for certain territorial concessions. Other agreements were reached at Yalta. Germany would be broken up into four occupation zones, administered one each by the United States, Britain, the Soviet Union, and France. Boundaries were to be adjusted after the war. A good deal of Polish territory would go to the Soviet Union. Poland would be compensated with lands to the west that formerly fell under the domain of Germany, and other borders in eastern and central Europe were to be adjusted.

More important than these painstakingly worked out adjustments to the map were the questions of who would govern Poland, and how. Here Stalin had a vision very different from that of the Western Allies. But now, at Yalta, neither Stalin nor Roosevelt nor Churchill was eager to tackle the problem head-on. Stalin went along happily with Roosevelt's and Churchill's insistence that free elections take place in Poland. The Yalta Conference ended with a "Declaration on Liberated Europe" that affirmed the need for democratic institutions in the postwar world.

The mood at Yalta bordered on jubilation; never again would relations of the wartime allies seem so rosy. The declaration to emerge from the conference was a document of great principle. But it had no teeth, and the Americans at Yalta who felt that Stalin would abide by the letter of the agreement were soon bitterly disappointed. Within a few months, the United States was forced to accept a Soviet-dominated government in Poland, and the chances for democratic elections throughout Eastern Europe seemed dim.

Before the conflict of views over plans for the new Europe became a major story in Washington, London, and Paris, President Roosevelt died, an event that saddened people around the world. On April 12, 1945, less than a month before Germany surrendered, a bespectacled former haberdasher and former senator from Missouri, Vice President Harry S Truman, took over the reins of power at the White House. It was Truman who would lead the West in the first years of the yet unnamed struggle between West and East.

How would the new president, essentially an unknown entity in the world of foreign affairs, deal with the wily Soviets on the partition of Poland? on the fate of vanquished Germany? on the critical question of elections in the conquered territories? The president's foreign-policy advisers offered the Missourian conflicting advice: James V. Forrestal, the secretary of the navy, advocated playing it tough: "We had better have a showdown now than later" was his counsel.[5] Secretary of War Henry L. Stimson, a man soon to be recognized as the intellectual father of the American foreign-policy elite, favored a more cautious approach: Forcing the Soviets' hand in Eastern Europe would only make it more difficult to reach acceptable compromises elsewhere.

Truman's early actions suggest that he leaned to the Forrestal position. The straight-talking chief executive had little patience for Moscow's tendency to agree to abide by principles and then, in its actions, ignore them without blinking. He gave Soviet Foreign Minister Vyacheslav Molotov a bitter tongue-lashing over Soviet delays in preparing for free elections in Poland and issued toughly worded proclamations, both oral and written, on what he thought of the Communists.

Meanwhile, the fighting against Japan continued. At the Potsdam (Germany) Conference, held from July 17 to August 2, 1945, the new president fenced with Stalin over the nature of the proposed Soviet intervention against the Japanese and about the details of the Allied administration in Germany. It was clear from the outset that the two men had vastly different visions of how the defeated nation should be treated. Truman's position was that a demilitarized Germany should be redeveloped and eventually made economically self-sufficient. The German people, known for their industriousness, discipline, and order, had not all been die-hard Nazis, and they could make a real contribution to the postwar world. Stalin, on the other hand, pressed hard to obtain rights to much of the German manufacturing equip-

ment, almost all of which was in the heavily industrialized parts of Germany which were now in Western
hands. He seemed to want to strip the nation of all its
remaining wealth, in part to replace the huge Soviet
losses suffered at the hands of the Nazis.

After much acrid debate, it was agreed that in
exchange for supplying foodstuffs (from the more agri-
culturally oriented Soviet-controlled eastern part of
Germany) to support the population in the western part
of Germany, Stalin would receive roughly twenty-five
percent of the capital (industrial) equipment then located in the western sectors. No permanent solution surfaced to the general question of the divided Germany.
After Potsdam, each of the Western countries and the
Soviets independently developed its region of German
territory. The Potsdam Conference, it appeared, had
deepened the American president's mistrust of the
Soviets. After returning to Washington, Truman private-
ly resolved never to let the Russians have any part in the
control of Japan, which had officially surrendered to the
United States in September 1945, after two of its cities
were destroyed by atomic bombs in early August. Stalin,
meanwhile, resented the Western powers for not appre-
ciating the extent of Soviet suffering at the hands of the
Germans. Attitudes were hardening on both sides.

In the United States these developments were looked
upon with frustration and even fear by a growing chorus
of people who could not see why their nation, having
secured victory in a great war, could not somehow put
the Russians in their place.

Stalin, for his part, did nothing to placate the West's

concerns that the Soviets had designs not only on Eastern Europe but on the Middle East as well. In early 1946, Soviet troops refused to leave the oil-rich province of Azerbaijan, despite having agreed to do so by the end of 1945. U.S. Secretary of State James F. Byrnes lodged a strong protest that was widely supported around the world. Diplomatic pressure from the newly formed United Nations organization led to a Soviet agreement to withdraw. It was also announced that a joint Soviet-Iranian company had been formed, subject to the approval of the Iranian parliament. In the end the withdrawal was completed, but the Iranian governing body dealt the Russians a serious defeat by failing to approve the joint venture.

In August of the same year came another threatening gesture: The Soviets demanded from Turkey shared control of the strategically important Dardanelles, the narrow strait connecting the Sea of Marmara and the arm of the Mediterranean Sea known as the Aegean Sea. The Turks, however, refused to give up control of the strait, which flows through their country and is part of the vital waterway linking the Black Sea and the Mediterranean Sea. When a U.S. Navy aircraft carrier steamed toward the strait to show United States support for the Turkish position, the Soviets backed down. Stalin was out to take what he could, but he was, in these early years of the conflict with the West, anxious to take it without going to war.

The run at the Dardanelles came just a few months after Winston Churchill weighed in with one of the most famous speeches of cold war history. Delivered at

Westminster College in Fulton, Missouri, with President Truman in attendance, the speech in many ways expressed the sentiments of the key decision makers in the U.S. government. It was a speech with a haunting and foreboding message. Above all else, it was memorable. Churchill declared the following:

> A shadow has fallen upon the scene so lately lighted up by the Allied victory. From Stettin in the Baltic, to Trieste in the Adriatic, an Iron Curtain has descended across the Continent. Behind that line lie all the capitals of the ancient states of Central and Eastern Europe. . . . [A]ll lie in what I must call the Soviet sphere. . . . Police governments are prevailing. . . . In front of the Iron Curtain . . . and through the world, Communist fifth columns [groups of secret sympathizers who engage in espionage and subversion] are established and work in complete unity and absolute obedience to the directions they receive from the Communist center. . . .[6]

The Iron Curtain speech angered Stalin. It fed his fears that the United States and Britain were conspiring against him, attempting to have their way everywhere, even in the territories that mattered the most to his country—those that bordered the Soviet Union. He remarked at one point that Churchill's speech amounted to a call to war with his country. The Soviet leader, concerned about the possibility of Western rearming of Germany, moved to isolate himself further from his former allies. He rejected Soviet membership in the World

Bank (a new financial institution designed to finance the rebuilding of nations decimated by years of war), which would have required Stalin to provide more information about the condition of war-ravaged Russia than he was willing to release. As 1946 drew to a close, only the most naive idealists still believed that the postwar world would be shaped by a spirit of cooperation, not conflict.

CHAPTER TWO

THE U.S. RESPONSE: THE TRUMAN DOCTRINE AND THE MARSHALL PLAN

The cold war policies of the two superpowers in the early years were molded in response to real events and crises. Perceptions and educated guesses, however, also played a vital role in the process. Stalin's brutal but effective security police had eliminated open political dissent in most of Eastern Europe by 1947. That was a fact. That he sought, like Hitler, to dominate the world and destroy the existence of capitalist societies was a perception, but it was a very powerful perception, and one with certain ramifications. Truman and his band of foreign-policy advisers believed that Stalin fully intended to exploit any sign of Western weakness, that he stood ready to pounce on any piece of territory he thought vulnerable. This was an article of faith in Washington; all cold war policies, all cold war institutions (the State and War Departments foremost among them) took it as a premise.

Likewise, it was a fact that the Soviet Union was surrounded, in effect, by non-Communist powers. It was Stalin's perception, though, that the United States and its Western allies sought through "capitalist encirclement" to crush the Soviet Union and the political ideas it stood for. His viewpoint was soon elevated to an article of faith in the Kremlin, and all future Soviet foreign-policy decisions took this belief into account.

The events of 1947—the subject of this chapter—strengthened the overly negative perceptions in the minds of both parties. American foreign-policy makers, looking out at the postwar world, imagined it would become one of free, open societies, a world of nations trading on an open market through a stable system of international finance with the United States acting as the leading nation. This was the best way, they felt, to ensure that no nation would take up arms against another again. The idea was to give all countries a fair chance to prosper, and to establish guidelines and principles through international institutions such as the United Nations and its agencies to make sure that grievances were aired and addressed.

Even before the groundwork had been laid for such a system, economic and social unrest in Europe and elsewhere threatened to make its implementation impossible. In Italy and France, Communist parties flourished, as they took advantage of popular discontent over shortages of food, clothing, and fuel and the inability of the established governments to deliver quick remedies to the massive upheaval that the war had caused.

In Asia, the Japanese conquest of European colonies

and the subsequent World War II defeat of the Japanese by powers committed to self-rule had awakened strong nationalist sentiments. A brilliant revolutionary, Ho Chi Minh, who was primarily a nationalist and secondly a Communist, began a fight for Vietnamese independence from France. The Dutch battled Indonesians fighting for independence from the Netherlands. In the Middle East, Jewish settlers and Arabs in the British-run mandate of Palestine were fighting, and no one was certain whether the British would remain in power there.

Each and every trouble spot offered opportunities for communism. The United States was convinced that new tools must be developed—diplomatic, political, and military—to cope with the challenge. It was with this precarious situation in mind that President Truman announced to a joint session of Congress and to a nationwide radio audience on March 12, 1947, the doctrine that bears his name. The president asked for $400 million in military and economic aid for Greece and Turkey, two countries where, he claimed, Communist rebels were attempting to topple pro-Western governments.

Truman, in fact, exaggerated the threat—he felt he must to sell the novel idea of the policy. He stated: "I believe that it must be the policy of the United States to support free peoples who are resisting attempted subjugation by armed minorities and outside pressures."[1]

Although in the March 12 speech the president never said the "armed minorities" were Communists, no one at the time of the speech or thereafter doubted that that was exactly what he meant. Undersecretary of State Dean Acheson, a devoted anti-Communist, defended the Truman Doctrine. He explained that the immediate aim of the Communist movement was the takeover of Greece. Should Greece be lost, Turkey would prove impossible to defend. If the Russians then pressed forward to take the Dardanelles, such a move would have, as Acheson put it, "the clearest implications" for the Middle East.[2] What the undersecretary meant was that if the Soviet Union succeeded in Greece and Turkey, it would be on its way to controlling the whole region. If the United States failed to show its resolve in Greece and Turkey, who could doubt that Soviet-sponsored pressure would be brought to bear in both Europe and Asia? Acheson was articulating an early version of something U.S. cold war planners would raise again and again in the coming decades: By the 1960s, it would be known as the domino theory. The idea was that if one country fell to communism, its neighbors were bound to topple, too.

Many congressmen were skeptical. They felt that the Truman Doctrine would open the door for direct United States involvement in trouble spots all over the globe. Acheson, however, was a persuasive and eloquent salesman, and the domino theory was hard to resist. The Congress approved not only the aid package but also the idea behind it. The Truman Doctrine promised aid (primarily military aid) to pro-Western regimes under Communist attack from within or without.

Military aid, however, was hardly sufficient to put Europe back on its feet. Something stronger was needed. The Truman administration's solution was the creative Marshall Plan, one of the most generous and farsighted foreign-aid policies in all history. General George Catlett

Marshall, Truman's able and wise secretary of state, first presented it in his Harvard University commencement address in June 1947.

In that seminal speech, Marshall urged the nations of Europe to produce a collective plan of economic recovery. The plan, once formulated, would then be submitted to the United States for approval and financing. The United States and Europe would together undertake a gargantuan public works project: the rebuilding of Western Europe.

Over the course of the next few months, Europeans and Americans, in a series of conferences, hammered out the details of the rebuilding process. It took the Democratic Truman administration several months to present its program to a budget-conscious Republican Congress. With great skill and subtlety, Marshall and his aides succeeded in convincing the majority of America's lawmakers that the Marshall Plan was indispensable to the development of a secure and prosperous postwar world. With few reservations, Congress agreed to fund the program.

Rebuilding of European factories, rail lines, roads, and bridges began immediately. And more work lay ahead. Over the course of the Marshall Plan's life—its projects were still running a decade after its inception—the U.S. taxpayer provided $17 billion in grants and loans to rebuild destroyed Europe between 1948 and 1952 alone. It was the largest international rescue mission ever devised. And it was a great success.

More than generosity had inspired the Marshall Plan. Economists warned that unless something was done to stimulate European demand for American goods, the U.S. economy might slide back into a recession or, worse, another depression. Millions of American businesses, recently recovered from the Great Depression, could again stumble into bankruptcy. Time was running out. Europe had suffered two frigid winters in a row and was on the verge of complete economic collapse. Secretary of State Marshall, impatient with the slow pace of the Allied efforts to put Europe back on its feet—there was still a great deal of bickering behind the scenes with the Soviets—remarked that the patient was sinking while the doctors deliberated.

The Americans had another reason to see that the plan took hold. The size and power of the French and Italian Communist Parties were formidable, which greatly worried Washington; but a strong Europe would be able to withstand the destabilizing influence of Communist subversion from within. A strong Europe could field a strong army, which would, in turn, make Western Europe a less inviting target for the Red Army.

Moscow's reaction to the Marshall Plan was, if nothing else, direct. *Pravda*, the most prominent Soviet newspaper, labeled the program a "Truman Doctrine with dollars." Stalin had seen the Truman Doctrine as a sort of minor declaration of war against communism generally and his country in particular. To the Russians, the Marshall Plan was more of the same.

Or was it? Marshall actually extended the offer of aid to the Soviet Union and Eastern Europe, and Foreign Minister Molotov showed up in Paris for discussions with the other European powers and the Americans. But coming up with a cooperative plan would have required the USSR to open its financial records. Stalin was not about to do that for anyone, even if it meant the Soviet people had to starve. In the end, Molotov and his team, angry and disturbed by the American "imperialists," stormed out of the discussions, not to return.

Soon afterward, Moscow announced its own "Molotov Plan," which speeded up the process of linking the Eastern European economies to that of the USSR. The Kremlin stepped up the intensity of its invective against the Western powers in general and against the United States in particular. The new propaganda campaign that was leveled at Washington hammered away at one theme: the Americans were conspiring to control Europe. Andrey Zhdanov, a truly hard-line member of the Politburo (the small group of ten to fifteen men who led the Soviet Union), figured prominently in the campaign. He said in a speech that "just as in the past the Munich policy* untied the hands of the Nazi aggressors, so today concessions to the new course of the United States and the imperialist camp may encourage its inspirers to be even more insolent and aggressive."[3]

Soon after the announcement of the Marshall Plan, Stalin moved to consolidate his power in Eastern Europe. He cracked down on Hungary, until then the most independent of all the Eastern European nations. The Soviet dictator ordered the secret police to rig the August 1947 Hungarian elections, which they did. It

*At the German city of Munich in 1938, Britain and France had agreed to cede part of Czechoslovakia to Hitler's Germany in the vain hope of averting a general war with Germany.

surprised no one when Zhdanov, who took a very dim view of the West, suddenly took on great prominence in "helping" to run the Hungarian government.

No one observed the Soviet reaction to those two ambitious American initiatives, the Truman Doctrine and the Marshall Plan, more carefully than George F. Kennan, one of the State Department's most able Sovietologists. Kennan, who had played an important part in formulating the Marshall Plan, was a man of great integrity, piercing insight, and literary skill. His "long telegram" of February 1946 concerning Soviet intentions and U.S. policy toward the Soviet Union had caused a sensation among the foreign-policy establishment in Washington. Secretary of the Navy Forrestal made the text required reading for all his high-ranking officers, and it was not long before the ideas Kennan outlined on Soviet conduct and American strategy gained wide acceptance.

These views were expressed in somewhat more detail in "The Sources of Soviet Conduct," an article Kennan published in the July 1947 issue of the prestigious journal *Foreign Affairs*. He described the Soviet leadership's deep-seated insecurity and traced its origins to Russia's czarist history: The Russians had gradually taken over neighboring states in order to diminish opportunities for invasion by the Western powers.*

*Indeed, the history of Russia had been a history of expansion. The Duchy of Muscovy under Ivan III had conquered many of its neighboring principalities in the sixteenth century; Peter the Great, who reigned alone from 1689 to 1725, acquired Estonia and parts of Finland in his effort to make Russia a maritime power; and Catherine the Great, who ruled from 1762 to 1796, obtained huge expanses of land from Poland and Turkey.

There was, Kennan posited, a "highly intimate" connection between Russian history and Communist ideology. The czars had sometimes tried to shape Russia into a Western nation, but there was a strong strand of antipathy to all things Western, just as there was in Soviet communism. Kennan believed that Russian history and Communist ideology reinforced one another. Thus, some degree of conflict between the USSR and the capitalist West was inevitable.

Stalin, the American diplomat went on to argue, could justify both his domestic repression and his domination of Eastern Europe as a necessary response to Western efforts to encircle the Soviet state. The czars had offered their people similar justifications for making the sacrifices required by the building of the Russian empire. Kennan's description of Soviet intentions in world affairs had it that the "Kremlin's political action is a fluid stream which moves constantly, wherever it is permitted to move, toward a given goal. Its main concern is that it has filled every nook and cranny available to it in the basin of world power."[4]

Given the Russian propensity to "fill every nook and cranny" and given the formidable obstacles in the way of that nation's joining the open societies of the West, how could the United States best handle the Soviets? Kennan suggested that American policy be centered on "the adroit and vigilant application of counter-force at a series of constantly shifting geographical and political points, corresponding to the shifts and maneuvers of Soviet policy."[5] In other words, the West should not attempt to liberate those areas already under Russian dominance, nor should it withdraw from the areas susceptible to Communist influence. The idea was to use whatever tools and resources were available—diplomatic, economic, military—to *contain* communism within its current sphere.

Unlike many members of the foreign-policy establishment, Kennan never believed the Soviets had plans to invade Western Europe. But he shrewdly (in light of Soviet actions from 1947 to 1990) foresaw that the Communists stood ready to take advantage of any opening given them by the Western powers. He stressed the importance of developing a prosperous Western Europe—one weakness the Soviets would surely exploit was a prostrate and unhappy populace—and he encouraged the United States to exploit the inevitable differences among the various Communist states and parties. If the open societies were patient, if they resisted Soviet efforts to expand, Kennan counseled, the whole Marxist-Leninist system would over time be discredited and collapse of its own weight.

Kennan's idea, called (sensibly enough) containment, was soon widely accepted among American foreign-policy experts in Washington. And though Kennan himself often complained that United States policy makers misunderstood his views, containment remained the cornerstone of American policy in fighting the cold war for the next forty years.

George F. Kennan left government service in the early 1950s, in large measure because he felt that government policy put too much emphasis on the military aspect of containment. There was some truth to his complaint. Certainly Truman's initial responses to the Soviet challenge did focus on military and security measures.

Among those initial responses was the National Security Act of July 1947, which created a new Department of Defense to coordinate the operation of America's vast and ever more complex armed services. Now that the atomic bomb was such a critical entity in world politics, it made sense to enhance the visibility of American air power; a separate U.S. Air Force was created (the Air Corps had been a branch of the U.S. Army). Out of the small and unorthodox Office of Strategic Services, the official United States espionage agency in World War II, came the Central Intelligence Agency (CIA). As the chief gatherer of information on Soviet capabilities and intentions and on Communists everywhere, the CIA played an enormous—some would say overly large—role in the great rivalry between the two superpowers.

The Department of Defense and the CIA were the key American cold war institutions. They required personnel, new equipment, and a great deal of funding. The Truman administration's proposed 1948 budget for defense was, in fact, the highest in the history of the nation in peacetime. The Republican isolationists—that is, those who thought it unwise for the United States to spend its energies and time in foreign affairs—were somewhat reluctant to embark on such an expensive crusade, and they told the president so. They were being asked to bail Europe out of the last war and to take a strong stand against the Soviet Union before it had moved to conquer a single acre of territory in either Western Europe or Asia.

The president, facing considerable opposition to his

new strategy for dealing with communism, tried to scare Congress into submission. On Capitol Hill his hand-picked generals and admirals on the newly formed Joint Chiefs of Staff spoke gravely of the lack of U.S. preparedness to meet Red challenges posed in Europe. Walter Bedell Smith, ambassador to the Soviet Union, reported in the winter of 1947–1948 that the Russians were hard at work on their own atomic bomb and a strategic air force to deliver those deadly weapons thousands of miles from Soviet borders.

Then, just as the effort to sell the big defense budget was under way, in February 1948, an event occurred that ensured that the defense appropriations would be forthcoming. The twelve non-Communists in Czechoslovakia's fledgling coalition government mysteriously resigned, soon after a not-so-friendly visit from a deputy foreign minister of the Soviet Union. On February 25, a new government of Czechoslovakia was formed—without even a semblance of any sort of free election. The new government was completely controlled by loyal Communists. Two weeks later, Jan Masaryk, the popular former foreign minister and a man of democratic principles, "fell" out of a window in Prague.

The reaction across the United States was one of shock. Czechoslovakia, a forward-looking democratic country, had, it appeared, been forcibly drawn into the Soviet camp. Not only had the United States failed to see it coming, it could do little to reverse the loss. Dread of more takeovers spread across Europe and the United States, and there was a genuine fear of war.

Stalin's actions in Czechoslovakia, and his utter disregard for the agreements regarding Eastern Europe that he had signed at Yalta and elsewhere during and right after World War II, shook the doubting Thomases in the Western powers and greatly accelerated the pace of Western efforts to check future Soviet adventures. On March 14, 1948, the Senate gave its full and final endorsement to the Marshall Plan. The vote wasn't even close (sixty-nine to seventeen). Two days later, Britain, France, and the Benelux countries (Belgium, the Netherlands, and Luxembourg), fearing the worst, signed the Brussels Treaty, which called upon the signatories to come to the aid of member nations in the event of an attack. Stalin saw the treaty as yet another indication that his former allies were plotting against him. But he was going to wait, wait just a little while, before testing their will to stand up to further Soviet pressure.

CHAPTER THREE

FROM THE BERLIN AIRLIFT TO THE "LOSS" OF CHINA

T he crisis in Czechoslovakia confirmed the need for a coherent American strategy to fend off Soviet expansionism. It also helped to legitimize containment, especially for a group of men in the United States who played a pivotal role in the cold war from beginning to end, despite their tendency to stay clear of elective office. They are known to historians as the "foreign-policy establishment."

It was not an establishment in the formal sense of belonging to any one institution or formal group. Wealth was no guarantee of membership in this exclusive club. It didn't hurt to have money, but other things seemed to be more important. Two of its most illustrious members were scions of the Protestant clergy. Dean Acheson, who served as Truman's undersecretary of state, and later (1949–1953) as secretary of state, had the right background and the proper credentials. He had gone to the prestigious Groton School and then to Yale and Harvard.

John Foster Dulles, a consultant to the State Department during the Truman years, was the Republican Party's chief expert on foreign policy. Like Acheson, he was trained as a lawyer. After Princeton and law school at George Washington University, he went to work for an important New York law firm. Dulles had an abiding, unshakable faith in the righteousness of the American cause in the cold war, and he often spoke of the growing rivalry between the Soviet Union and the United States as if it were a struggle between God and the Devil.

Acheson; Dulles; John J. McCloy, the high commissioner of Germany after the war; Robert A. Lovett, undersecretary of state, later secretary of defense, and key adviser to John F. Kennedy in the 1960s—all had attended renowned Eastern colleges. All had experience in powerful law offices or banking institutions. Moreover, these were men, observed the British historian Godfrey Hodgson, "who came from a tradition of service and who possessed a certain confidence that the ways of power were open to them. They were defined by a history, a policy and an aspiration."[1]

The history that defined these men was World War II, where they had played critical roles in shaping and monitoring the vast U.S. industrial machine mobilized to defeat the Germans and the Japanese. They had all worked on the complicated transition from a wartime economy to a peacetime economy. Their policy was one of opposition to isolationism at home and to communism abroad. They aspired to nothing less than the moral and political leadership of the world. It was their style, wrote Hodgson,

> to deprecate chauvinism [excessive pride in one's country], while at the same time pressing for American wishes to be respected and American strength felt, around the world; to advocate restraint, and yet to despise softness and to admire a willingness to use military power; to feel conscience, but by no means to allow it to paralyze one into inaction; to walk softly with one's big stick, but to be ready to crack heads with it.[2]

The foreign-policy establishment was nonpartisan; it was peopled with Democrats, Republicans, and independents. Their power was exercised through the executive branch: the president appointed them. These men viewed public opinion in foreign policy not so much as a force to be respected but as something to be molded to fit the imperatives of a democratic superpower in a very dangerous age.

A pressing issue facing President Truman and the foreign-policy establishment in the wake of the Communist coup in Czechoslovakia was how to redress the grave imbalance of conventional armed forces in Europe. The Soviets had about twenty well-equipped divisions on the frontier between East and West (mostly in the Soviet-occupied zone in eastern Germany) in early 1948. The West had less than half that number of divisions, and they were neither as well trained nor as well equipped as the Russians. Soon the European signatories of the Brussels Treaty were talking with Robert A. Lovett and other U.S. representatives about the possibility of direct participation in a planned alliance soon to be known as the North Atlantic Treaty Organization (NATO).

Negotiations for the first peacetime military alliance in U.S. history were overshadowed by developments concerning the future of Germany. The Western powers, particularly France, had no intention of rearming Germany. Yet no one could deny that if Western Europe was to recover fully in the postwar era, Germany must play a vital economic role. That led to an agreement among the Western powers to lay the groundwork for a separate West German state, with a government friendly to the United States, the United Kingdom (Britain), and France but independently governed by the Germans themselves.

For the Soviet Union, this plan had dire implications. First of all, it established (at least in the minds of the Soviets) that France and Britain were overcoming their fear of a revived Germany; these governments were, in other words, accepting the United States' view that a healthy Europe was impossible without an independent German state. It escaped no one's notice, least of all Stalin's, that the Americans would eventually press their allies for a *rearmed* West German state. Indeed, it was hard to imagine how the Europeans and Americans could create a long-term deterrent to the massive Soviet Red Army without a strong German army.

The Western powers were well aware of Soviet anxi-

eties over a rearmed Germany, but they went ahead any-
way, undaunted by ominously worded statements from
Moscow claiming that the imperialists were threatening
world peace. In June the Western countries took another
step toward the creation of an independent Germany:
They issued a new currency, the deutsche mark—a sure
sign that the West had no intention of seeing a united
and "neutralized" Germany that might fall under the
sway of the Eastern bloc, as the Soviet Union and Soviet-
dominated Eastern Europe were now being called.

The Russians, whose objective had been to negotiate
for a united Germany over which they would be able to
exercise at least some control, were incensed. Vasily D.
Sokolovsky, who held the high military rank of marshal,
a type of Soviet general, called the issuance of the new
currency illegal and demanded that the West continue
to negotiate a reunification settlement. The Western
Allies demurred: The Soviet army could trample on the
freedoms of the peoples to the east of the Elbe. But they
were not going to do so to the west of that river, considered the boundary between the Communist- and
Western-held regions of Germany. Nor would they do so
in West Berlin, which (despite its location inside eastern
Germany) was to be run exclusively by the Western
powers according to previous agreements between the
Soviets and the West.

On June 24, 1948, the Soviets shut down the railway
and all highways leading from the Western-occupied
zones of Germany to the Western-controlled sectors of
the former capital of Hitler's Reich, the city of Berlin.
When pressed for an explanation—the shutdowns were

blatant violations of wartime agreements among the great powers—the Soviets claimed they had power shortages and damaged railroad beds. These were outright lies. Everyone in Europe and the United States knew it. The Russians were sending a very strong signal to the Western Allies: Western access to the 2.4 million inhabitants of the three Western sectors of Berlin was not inviolable. If the West wanted to play tough when it came to questions concerning German unification, then the Soviets could play even tougher when it came to Berlin. And so began the Berlin Blockade, the first of the great crises of the cold war.

What was Stalin up to, and why? The Soviet leader recognized that his country was facing severe challenges. The Marshall Plan would help Western Europe recover more rapidly than the Soviet Union or its satellite nations. The Brussels Treaty was not in itself a direct military threat to the USSR; it would be years before the West had a credible conventional force that could challenge the Red Army's power on the ground. But with the entry of the United States into the European alliance (although not accomplished officially until 1949) the Soviet Union would face further encirclement in the form of air and naval bases. To compound Soviet difficulties, the Communist leader in Yugoslavia, Josip Broz Tito, was unwilling to play his assigned role: that of Stalin's puppet. The Soviet dictator tried to topple the Yugoslav ruler via the usual Russian means—the use of the secret police (known by different names at different times, the most common being the initials KGB)—but he succeeded only in greatly increasing Tito's popularity.

In short, Stalin needed some sort of victory in this new and very important rivalry with the West, and he probably reasoned that the Americans, the British, and the French would see that in the matter of West Berlin's freedom, they had few cards to play. They couldn't very well take on the Red Army directly and force their way through to West Berlin. Nor did Stalin, or anyone else in the Kremlin, think it possible for the West to supply Berlin with food, electricity, and coal for heating without access by road, train, or waterway.

But Stalin misjudged Western resolve. General Lucius Clay, military governor of the U.S. sector of Berlin, wired the White House, claiming that failure to hold the line in Berlin would lead to Russian control of all Germany. There were, after all, written agreements guaranteeing Western access to the city by air. It would be a tough job to keep West Berlin afloat, but it was the only option short of surrender or all-out war.

So began the Berlin Airlift. All over the city, day and night, the drone of World War II–era bombers and transports could be heard, bringing in vast quantities of milk, cereal, eggs, blankets, coal, and electric generators. Air force personnel, both British and American, were flown in from all over the world to participate in the herculean mission.

Over the ensuing weeks, the rescue effort increased in power and efficiency. Soon, four thousand tons a day were being flown into Gatlow and Templehof airports in the Western sector of Berlin. At peak periods, a plane either took off or landed every ninety seconds.

The Soviets, surprised and dismayed that their

strong-arm tactics hadn't forced the Western powers to give in, agreed to discussions in July 1948. Settlement of the Berlin question, Stalin made it clear, was dependent on "the general question of four-power control in regard to Germany."[2] The United States didn't buy it. It would not be bullied into negotiating.

In mid-July, President Truman sent a signal of his own by ordering to British airfields two squadrons of B-29s fully capable of carrying nuclear bombs. Negotiations continued into the fall of 1948, by which time it was obvious that the West could and would supply the West Berliners indefinitely. The longer the airlift lasted, the less leverage Stalin had.

Finally, on May 12, 1949, the Soviet Union quietly lifted the Berlin Blockade. All that Stalin received in exchange was a promise to continue discussions about postwar Germany. Unfortunately for the Soviet Union, however, the blockade had evaporated whatever little desire there had been to settle the German question in light of the Soviets' anxieties about their historical adversaries, the Germans.

On May 23, 1949, a dark day for Moscow, the Federal Republic of Germany (usually referred to as West Germany) was born.* In July, after an energetic defense of the NATO alliance by Secretary of State Dean Acheson, the U.S. Senate approved full American membership in the pact. NATO, also known as the Atlantic Alliance, formally united the nations of Western Europe with the United States and Canada in a commitment to mutual

*The Soviets responded by forming the German Democratic Republic (East Germany) in October of that year.

security. The parties to the treaty agreed that an armed attack against one nation would be considered an attack against them *all.*

All of this was good news for Truman and his foreign-policy advisers, and a great setback for the Soviets. But the United States was about to experience some setbacks of its own. President Truman announced to the public on September 23 that the Soviet Union had recently exploded its first atomic bomb. The American atomic monopoly had disappeared, and with it, some measure of European and American security. Truman called for the acceleration of the development of the hydrogen bomb, a far more powerful weapon than the atomic bombs used on the Japanese cities of Hiroshima and Nagasaki, and serious talks began in Washington about rearming the Germans (somewhat to the dismay of the French, who had been invaded by Germany twice in the twentieth century). And then, just a week later, another devastating blow: Nationalist China, a government that had long enjoyed the support of the United States, fell to the Communists under Mao Zedong.

The "loss" of China, as the newspapers of the day put it, had not been entirely unexpected in Washington, but this hardly softened the blow in cities and towns across the United States. The chief of the American advisory group in China had warned of trouble in late 1948. Chiang Kai-shek, the leader of Nationalist China, whom the Americans funded and supported, had more than his share of problems. His army was disintegrating; his government was corrupt and without direction. Chiang had never been able to accept that his survival depended on extensive administrative reforms and the elimination of corruption among his army officer corps.

U.S. policy toward China in the 1930s and 1940s sought to strengthen the hand of the Nationalists, who found themselves in a savage, drawn-out civil war against Mao Zedong. Mao, a charismatic leader with legions of loyal followers, preached the language of Communist revolution and reform.

By the end of World War II, the Communists had seized control of land with about one quarter of the Chinese population, the largest of any nation on earth. Efforts by the United States (among others) to create a coalition government, with power shared between the two political factions and their armies, came to a bad end, and a new round of fighting broke out. By early February 1949, the Communists had wrested control of all Manchuria from the Nationalist forces, who lacked the training and motivation of the Communist army.

The initial response of the Truman administration to the impending collapse of the Nationalist government had been cool and realistic: the United States should cut off aid and begin to distance itself from the doomed Nationalists. Dealing with Chiang had been, at best, an exercise in frustration. It was clear soon after the end of World War II that he was not the catalyst the Chinese people needed to implement the vast social and economic changes required to bring their country into the modern world.

By the end of 1949, what was left of Chiang's army, along with Chiang himself, limped off the mainland to set up its own separate Chinese Nationalist government on the island of Formosa (Taiwan), which is located off China's southeastern coast. Once the Nationalists had left the mainland, Dean Acheson suggested that a stronger China under Mao might not be a thorn in the side of American policy in Asia. Perhaps Mao's strong nationalism would assert itself, and China, too, might serve to restrain the Soviet Union's expansionist tendencies.

Acheson's outlook reflected his knowledge of power politics. Ideology was not the ultimate factor in distinguishing friend from foe. Even a *Communist* China could have strategic interests that corresponded to those of the West. Acheson was right, but that didn't matter to an American public that had been told, and told repeatedly, that communism was the greatest threat to peace on earth. A great country, with a long and established relationship with the United States, had "gone Red," fallen under the spell of Stalin's disciple Mao.

In Washington the Republican-led "China Lobby" intoned against the Truman administration's loss of China. It was a ridiculous charge, rooted as it was in the idea that the United States had the power to stop upheavals of such complexity when it was having a tough time managing the "first line" of defense in Western Europe. A foolish notion, but many believed it. Thus it was that a wave of paranoia about Communist infiltration in the United States, and more particularly in the U.S. government, began to rise. (About this we will have much more to say in Chapter five.)

There were other ramifications. The United States now spoke with a less unified voice in world affairs, as bitterness and acrimony infused congressional debates and discussions over future efforts to check communism in Asia. Containment, it now appeared, was both more complex and more baffling than most had thought.

This series of crises in 1949—first Berlin, then the Soviet atomic bomb, then the addition of China to the Communist bloc—led to a full-scale reassessment of foreign policy in the corridors of Washington. President Truman directed an ad hoc committee of diplomats, defense experts, and policy analysts to ponder these basic questions: What were the main threats to national security? How could the nation best mobilize its energies to prevent the expansion of Soviet influence, while at the same time extending the boundaries of the democratic world in the Middle East, in Africa, in Europe?

The report that emerged from the group's discussions, called National Security policy document sixty-eight (or NSC-68 for short) was undeniably one of the most significant documents of the cold war. It served as a guidepost and premise for Republican and Democratic administrations for the next twenty years, and it lost its relevance only after the nation was deeply embroiled in a war against communism in Vietnam.

Paul H. Nitze, who succeeded George Kennan as the leader of the State Department's policy-planning staff, was NSC-68's principal author. He turned the paper over to President Truman in April 1950. Nitze took a dim view of Soviet intentions and capabilities around the world—much dimmer, in fact, than did Kennan. Global stability seemed to Nitze a very tenuous thing: "The assault on free institutions is worldwide now,

and in the context of the present polarization of power a defeat of free institutions anywhere is a defeat everywhere."[3]

Threats of such overwhelming magnitude required a drastic and rapid response. If the United States was to create an international environment based on democratic governments and free trade, then vigilance was of the utmost importance. The means to counter any Communist threat, wherever it reared up, was essential. Atomic weaponry and the threat of overwhelming destruction would not be sufficient to curb the expansionist appetites of the Soviet Union and its satellite states. It was important, concluded NSC-68, "to increase as rapidly as possible our general air, ground and sea strengths and that of our allies to a point where we are militarily not so dependent on atomic weapons."[4]

In reading over the document, Truman and his advisers were surely struck by the divergent outlooks of Nitze and Kennan. George F. Kennan, who had first outlined what containment was all about, felt it foolish and beyond the capability of the United States to counter *any* threat *anywhere*. The father of containment had argued that the United States should make it clear that any Soviet move against the major strategic-industrial centers—Western Europe, Japan, Britain, the North American continent—would not be tolerated. He never felt that any Communist move anywhere should be countered with force. Kennan had also repeatedly indicated that the Soviets were unlikely to launch a major offensive in Western Europe.

NSC-68 endorsed a far more pessimistic picture,

even suggesting that failure to expand U.S. military forces quickly would render the West helpless when the Soviets made their move. The Nitze document also predicted that after 1954 the USSR would have the capacity to destroy the United States with a well-stocked arsenal of nuclear weapons. In order to address the problem, the United States would have to spend about $35 billion a year for defense, an inconceivable sum, considering the country wasn't at war—at least not at war in the traditional sense.

NSC-68 can easily be read as a reaction to the chain of statements and actions emanating from the Kremlin. Stalin scared people. (He obviously had Nitze worried.) The Soviet position on Eastern Europe, the takeover in Czechoslovakia, the Berlin Blockade all seemed to confirm that the cold war was not just another power struggle between two great powers, but a moral crusade in which the United States was "good" and the Soviet Union "evil."

Taking the moral high ground, as American statesmen did in NSC-68 and throughout the cold war, created additional problems and may very well have increased the already huge number of problems with which the superpowers had to deal. Not the least of these was that it blinded the Americans, prevented them from seeing the world from the Kremlin's point of view. It never seems to have occurred to the authors of NSC-68, or to any other of the early key players in our story, that Moscow had every reason in the world to mistrust the Western powers and to see U.S. policy as essentially offensive in nature. The United States and the

West, Stalin rightly believed, were out to crush the Marxist-Leninist system before it had a chance to flower.

In any case, Harry Truman had never trusted the Russians. He appeared ready to dismiss the dispassionate views of George Kennan and to accept the argument put forward in the National Security policy document. Yet he was greatly concerned about the costs involved. As the president himself wrote, accepting NSC-68 meant "doubling or tripling the [defense] budget, increasing taxes heavily, and imposing various kinds of economic controls. It meant a great change in our normal peacetime way of doing things."[5]

In the end Harry Truman didn't have to make a clear decision concerning the policy document. On June 25, 1950, not long after the final version of NSC-68 had landed on the president's desk, the army of North Korea, a close ally of Communist China, launched an invasion of pro-Western South Korea. The first "hot" war of the cold war was under way.

CHAPTER FOUR

WAR IN KOREA
1950–53

The Korean peninsula, which pushes out some six hundred miles from the Asian mainland, has been at the center of great power disputes for centuries. The Koreans, a fiercely independent people, have a common history and language dating back two thousand years. In the early twentieth century, the expansive Japanese empire had become the dominant political force in Korea; by 1910, the country was annexed by Japan. Thirty-five years of exploitation followed, during which all efforts by the Koreans and their allies to restore independence were mercilessly crushed.

The defeat of Japan in World War II meant that, once again, Koreans would run Korea. The question then was who would administer and monitor the transition period between the end of Japanese occupation and the formation of a popularly elected Korean government. The victorious Allied powers agreed to a simple formula: The Japanese would surrender to the Soviet troops north of the thirty-eighth parallel. The Red Army would administer there. To the south, Americans would take charge.

The division of Korea into two zones was never intended to be permanent; it had been undertaken as a matter of military expediency. Nevertheless, soon after the Japanese surrender, U.S. intelligence officers observed Soviet troops in North Korea building fortifications along the border. The message from the north was clear: If Korea was to be unified under one flag, it must have a government friendly to Soviet aspirations. Otherwise, what was the point of the fortifications?

Most experts in the United States had not envisioned Korea as a likely place for the cold war to turn hot. Most of the U.S. occupation troops had left the peninsula by 1948. Some of them had returned to Japan, where the United States was rapidly helping to rebuild that broken nation; others had returned home as part of the general downsizing of forces at the end of World War II (and a need to lower expenses in the federal budget). Rather than handle the delicate negotiations over Korean unification with the Soviets directly, the United States decided to turn the matter over to the United Nations. The Russians, however, wouldn't allow the UN commission access to the part of the country under their control. They were no more interested in holding fair elections to establish a single government throughout Korea than were their allies, the Communists in North Korea. By late 1948, two entirely distinct (and hostile) governments emerged: first, the Western-backed Republic of Korea in the south; then, the Soviet-sponsored Democratic People's Republic of Korea in the north.

By the spring of 1950, more than a year after Soviet troops had withdrawn from Korea, the North Koreans had developed an invasion plan to bring all Korea under their control. On the morning of June 25, almost assuredly with Soviet encouragement, the North Korean army launched a multidivision invasion of South Korea. Caught by surprise, the South Korean troops broke ranks and went into a disorderly retreat.

Why did the Communists undertake so audacious a move? Recent scholarship suggests that North Korean leader Kim Il-Sung thought his army capable of crushing the ill-equipped and unsuspecting South Korean army quickly, before that government's allies, particularly the United States, had time to react. North Korea's Premier Kim knew that American support for the authoritarian South Korean leader, Syngman Rhee, had always been somewhat reluctant. Then there was a famous speech in international relations circles, given before the National Press Club in January 1950, in which Secretary of State Acheson had excluded Korea from the "American defense perimeter."

Had the Americans read the attack as a simple case of civil war, they might have responded with strong words but no military action whatsoever. In fact, as historian (and Korean War combat veteran) Harry Summers has observed:

At the time it was assumed that "monolithic world communism," controlled and directed by Soviet

Premier Joseph Stalin in Moscow, was spreading by force of arms and that Korea was merely the first step in a communist plan for world conquest. It was this assumption, not the invasion of Korea itself, that triggered the strong reaction to North Korea's aggression. Applying the "lessons of Munich" [where appeasement of Hitler's seizure of part of Czechoslovakia led to even further Nazi aggression], the United Nations Security Council called upon all member nations to aid South Korea in resisting.[1]

On June 27, Truman announced that he was sending U.S. air and naval forces to Korea to provide support to the beleaguered South Korean troops. He also sent the Seventh Fleet to the Formosa Straits to prevent the spread of conflict. A few hundred soldiers stationed on the Japanese island of Kyushu were given orders on the morning of June 30: They would be the first Americans to assist the South Korean forces in their efforts to break the advance of the Communist troops. By July 2, the U.S. soldiers had taken up blocking positions to the north-east of the city of Taejon.

The 440 men of this first U.S. Army contingent, called Task Force Smith, were a mix of World War II veterans and young soldiers who had never seen battle. Poorly trained and softened by occupation duty in Japan, the GIs were in for a sobering experience. When the North Koreans approached the South's defensive positions, artillery fire failed to halt the oncoming enemy infantry. Their antitank weapons, of World War

II vintage, bounced ammunition harmlessly off the rugged T-34 tanks of Soviet manufacture. Task Force Smith quickly fell into disarray and panicked retreat.

Other, more seasoned American units soon made their way to the front, slowing the North Korean advance. In early August, a hastily assembled U.S. Army–South Korean defensive force took up positions within what was called the Pusan Perimeter, an area on the southeastern tip of the Korean Peninsula. The perimeter stretched a little more than one hundred miles north to south and about fifty miles east to west. The jewel of this small stake of ground was the port city of Pusan—the only place where reinforcements could be landed. It was touch-and-go for a few days, but the Pusan Perimeter held firm.

The blunting of the North Korean offensive marked the end of the first phase of the Korean War. The second phase of the conflict went considerably better for the UN forces. (The Americans contributed most of the troops and led the UN coalition of forces that challenged North Korea in the Korean War.) General Douglas MacArthur, hero of the Pacific Island–hopping campaign against the Japanese in World War II, head of the occupation forces in Japan, and one of best strategists in American military history, conceived and led an amphibious invasion into the heart of North Korea.

The Inchon landing, as the operation was called, was undertaken with considerable risk—more risk, in fact, than most such assaults. The formidable invasion force had been hastily assembled; disparate units from many nations had been quickly thrown together (although the vast majority were from the U.S. Army and Marines), leading to worries among the top brass that "command and control" of the units might break down. There was the matter of the tricky tides at Inchon. If there were delays and the tide dropped too far, the landing craft would be stranded and the troops would be at the mercy of the North Korean gunners defending the harbor.

MacArthur was not a man to be put off by risk. Thanks to great courage, inspired leadership, and a bit of luck, Inchon was a brilliant success. MacArthur's idea, which military strategists called strategic envelopment, had been to break in behind the southward-advancing North Korean troops, cutting off their supply lines. Then the UN forces that had held firm in the Pusan Perimeter would attack, forcing the North Koreans to reverse their course and driving the enemy soldiers northward into the positions held by UN forces spreading out from Inchon.

Less than two weeks after the September 15 amphibious landing at Inchon, MacArthur's troops had recaptured Seoul, the South Korean capital, and the North Koreans were on the run. By early October, the major UN objective had been achieved: The only North Koreans on South Korean soil were dead.

Neither Truman nor MacArthur, however, saw the ouster of the invading forces, despite early setbacks, as the end of the story. Indeed, the Americans had believed from the outset of hostilities that the Korean War was not solely about liberating South Korea. It was a cold war conflict, and it seemed plausible that, as one historian put it, "because early Soviet efforts to expand in Western Europe had been blocked by the American initiatives of 1947–48, Soviet policy had [with the advent of fighting in Korea] now entered a new, hard phase characterized by reliance on military force."[2]

Truman now faced another critical decision: Should he accept the *status quo ante bellum* (the situation as it had existed before the outbreak of war), or should a new strategy be devised with a more ambitious objective in mind?

The British prime minster, Clement Attlee, shuttled off to Washington, where he urged Truman not to take drastic action. Attlee feared, as did many in the great capitals of the world, that World War III was on the verge of breaking out. The Chinese had been sending very menacing signals to the Americans concerning U.S. actions in Korea. Beijing (the capital of China) had come close to threatening intervention should the United States persist in interfering. In Attlee's view, the Chinese were using Korea as an excuse, or cover, for a major assault on the West. Perhaps now was the time, he further suggested, to negotiate with the Chinese, to try to exploit whatever differences the Chinese had with the Soviets.

The American president didn't take the British prime minister's advice, although he did agree, at Attlee's request, to rule out the use of atomic weapons unless the UN forces were on the verge of being driven from the Korean peninsula entirely. Truman directed MacArthur to press forward. The new objective was the destruction of the North Korean armed forces. In the words newspapers used at the time, Communism was to be "rolled back." The UN General Assembly reinforced the U.S. president's directive with a resolution calling for UN troops to have "free and unhampered access to all parts of Korea." On October 9, 1950, the U.S. Army's First Cavalry Division crossed the thirty-eighth parallel into North Korea for the first time; they had marching orders to head for Pyongyang, the North Korean capital.

In undertaking this vastly more ambitious objective, Truman and the UN had reckoned that neither the Soviet Union nor Communist China, which had a long border with North Korea, would escalate the stakes through direct intervention. As it happened, the two Communist giants were quarreling with each other over certain territorial questions. When China's foreign minister, Zhou Enlai (also known as Chou En-Lai), warned the United Nations and the United States that China would not tolerate an invasion of its neighbor by imperialists, Truman and Acheson dismissed the threat as pure bluff.

And so MacArthur went forward. Splitting his forces roughly in half, he sent one army north via the east coast of Korea and one on the west coast, up to the Yalu River. At first, all proceeded as planned. Then came the great and unexpected blow: Around October 15, as the weather took a turn for the worse (Korea has very cold and unforgiving winters), 250,000 Communist Chinese Army "volunteers" began to cross the Yalu River, moving south into Korea to halt the UN drive northward.

The CCF (Communist Chinese Forces) caught the UN troops by surprise. Although the Chinese took heavy casualties from blistering UN firepower, by the end of

1950 they drove the UN forces out of North Korea and secured control of some South Korean territory, including Seoul. Following this rapid Communist Chinese advance, the UN armies pulled together, rallied, and drove the CCF back across the thirty-eighth parallel.

The new UN offensive, launched in late January 1951, did much to revive the tarnished reputation of the U.S. Army, which had initially performed poorly in Korea. It also reopened the question of the UN objectives: Should the war be fought to the finish? Should the fight be taken all the way to China? General MacArthur pressed to continue the fight. He called for Nationalist Chinese reinforcements from Taiwan, a bombing campaign directed against Chinese industrial centers and areas where troop concentrations could be detected by air reconnaissance, and a naval blockade of China's coast.

Truman disagreed with his field commander. He took Attlee's advice and the counsel of another World War II hero, General Omar N. Bradley, the chairman of the U.S. Joint Chiefs of Staff, who said that to challenge China would involve the United States "in the wrong war, at the wrong place, at the wrong time, and with the wrong enemy."[3] MacArthur refused to accept Truman's orders and tried to pressure the commander in chief to reverse his decision. He even took his disagreement to the press, hoping to pressure his president into reversing his decision not to widen the war.

The general's maneuverings led to one of the greatest and most publicized quarrels in American history between a general in the field and a commander in chief in Washington. In April 1951, MacArthur was relieved of command in Korea. The official reason was that he had made unauthorized policy statements that had, in effect, challenged the president's orders. The war settled into a stalemated conflict, not unlike World War I, with the two armies, UN (with forces from many nations, including Turkey, Britain, Australia, Canada, Belgium, and Greece, to name a few) on one side of the thirty-eighth parallel and the North Koreans and Chinese on the other. Thousands more died over the next two years as peace talks, carried out in Panmunjom, Korea, dragged on between the UN and the North Koreans and Chinese.

The end of the war in Korea came in the form of an armistice, signed on July 27, 1953, two years after the talks had begun. By that time, the American people had grown weary of the inconclusive conflict. For the Koreans themselves, it was the beginning of a long and uneasy peace. The demilitarized zone between the two nations remains today, and relations are at best chilly. In 1994, despite protest from around the world, North Korea appeared determined to produce its own nuclear weapon, but it finally agreed not to do so. Thousands of American soldiers are stationed in South Korea as a grim deterrent to North Korean adventurism, a reminder that traces of the old cold war world remain with us still.

It had been costly all around. American casualties were steep—more than 33,000 were killed in battle; another 20,000 died of illness and disease, including death from frostbite; more than 100,000 U.S. troops were wounded while serving in Asia. Other UN forces' losses totaled 3,000 men killed in battle and 11,000 wounded. It isn't known—at least the figures haven't been released—how many North Korean and Chinese soldiers perished. A fair guess is one million killed. Civilian casualties are also unknown, but because of the rapid movement of vast, modern armies and Korea's forbidding climate, they were excruciatingly high. Perhaps as many as two million Korean citizens died.

The Korean war has the dubious distinction of being America's "forgotten war." In terms of popular recognition, the term fits. Forgotten it may be; it was also, however, a conflict of immense significance. It convinced legions of people in the West that communism was bent on world domination. The initial invasion served to verify the fears of the most ardent anti-Communists in the United States: Moscow and Beijing were ready and willing to exploit Western lack of resolve. After attacking a nation friendly to the West, the Communists had come perilously close to gobbling up the entire Korean peninsula. And the reason for their success, in the minds of many in government at the time, was simple: lack of American vigilance.

Scholars now know that the Soviet role in the planning of the war was quite limited and that the invasion of June 1950 was not, in fact, the first step in a so-called Soviet master plan to dominate all Asia and then the world, as Washington had advertised. This information was not, of course, available to Harry Truman, his advisers, or anyone else in the West; so, given what they did know of

Communist ideas and outlook, it is hard to see how they could have responded differently.

The war in Korea established that the cold war would be more expensive for the Americans than they had previously imagined. It wasn't only Western Europe that the United States had apparently obligated itself to defend—it was Asia, too. After Korea, it was increasingly clear that the cold war would be fought outside Europe, in places that were beginning to be called developing nations and, later, the Third World. These societies shared a number of characteristics: Great poverty, political instability, and rising expectations for change were among the most prominent.

Truman, his advisers, and the foreign-policy establishment all agreed on one thing: The challenge of becoming the world's policeman meant the United States needed more tools to deter Communist ambition, and, if necessary, to challenge it directly. As the challenge was worldwide and would require the quick dispatch of forces, a larger, more diverse navy was required. If the distressing performance of the first U.S. troops in Korea was not to be repeated, more funds would be needed for the training of divisions that could respond quickly with great force.

It was clear that, as journalist Mel Elfin observed, the Korean War "transformed the Cold War from a political and ideological struggle into a military one. In so doing, it was a catalyst . . . for the creation of what Dwight D. Eisenhower [in 1961] dubbed 'the military-industrial complex.' Defense outlays soared from a planned $14 billion in 1951 to $54 billion in 1953."[4]

The Korean war also offered some hints about the complexity of warfare in a nuclear age. The MacArthur-Truman debate and the subsequent dismissal of the general had set off a firestorm of protest in the United States. In the world wars, it had been the Americans' policy to carry a fight to the enemy until the enemy was vanquished. In defense of his belief that the UN forces should press forward yet again to crush the Chinese Communists, MacArthur had invoked one of his most memorable statements: "In war there is no substitute for victory." The gut response of many in the United States had been to agree with the general.

Harry Truman, however, wisely recognized that the world had changed. In an age of nuclear weapons, in an age of containment, there was no room for all-out war. The dangers, the possibility of a miscue, were too great.

Korea was the first in a line of international conflicts called limited wars. Victory in these smaller conflicts was a shadowy thing, devilishly hard to define, orchestrate, and accomplish. The United States discovered that the hard way in Korea and, later on, in Vietnam.

Truman's decision not to unleash the full power of the U.S. military against the Chinese and North Koreans may very well have averted the outbreak of nuclear war. It also caused his popularity to plummet. Harry S Truman, the Democrat from Missouri and the cold war president, decided not to run for reelection in 1952. Dwight D. Eisenhower, "Ike," the World War II supreme commander in Europe, easily won election to the nation's highest office. Running as a Republican, he had promised to end the war in Korea. Given a little time, he did.

Ike had his own ideas about the threat the Soviets posed to the West and how the United States should conduct itself in this increasingly consuming rivalry. One of the many complications he faced in fashioning a cold war strategy for his administration concerned ugly developments over Communists, or supposed Communists, at home. By 1952, cynical American politicians were exploiting the public's growing fear of the Communist threat for their own ends. The McCarthy era was already well under way.

CHAPTER FIVE

THE COLD WAR AT HOME

So far, this account of the cold war has focused on the actions and policies of high-level government officials, particularly those of the United States and the Soviet Union. Presidents, premiers, secretaries of state, and their advisers were, of course, the architects of the superpower rivalry, but they were not the only people to feel its effects. By the early 1950s, the struggle against communism had become an obsession throughout the United States. Ordinary American citizens nervously pondered the future. They worried that the "evil forces" of communism might gain strength through conquest in Europe and Asia. They worried that Moscow would stop at nothing to achieve its dream of world domination and that the United States lacked the will and the might to resist. They worried, perhaps most of all, about their neighbors. Was Mr. Smith down the road a "true-blue American"? Was the college professor who lived next door a secret supporter of leftist ideas? Were there Communists masquerading as legitimate politicians, whose sole aim was the destruction of the system they had been elected to serve?

The fear of internal subversion was a chief characteristic of life in the late 1940s and early 1950s in the United States. There had been Red Scares in the 1920s and 1930s, but this new panic was far more pervasive than what had previously occurred. From the vantage point of the 1990s, it is clear that these widely felt fears were out of proportion to the size of the threat. But, as we have said, perceptions play a role in historical events, even when they diverge from reality. Americans living and working in the postwar era believed the threats were real.

The Red Scare that emerged in the late 1940s and early 1950s claimed thousands of innocent victims. Some were denied jobs; others, many of them veterans with long records of association with patriotic causes, lost their good reputations. With a depressing degree of regularity, courts upheld flimsy accusations in the name of preserving "national security."

The anti-Communist crusade had other dire effects on life in the United States. Opportunistic politicians preyed on the fears of voters to forward their own political fortunes, often smearing truth in the process. The atmosphere of suspicion and fear limited freedom of expression in the most egregious ways. An extraordinary amount of human energy was expended in leveling, investigating, and fighting disloyalty charges, the vast majority of which had no grounding in fact. Exactly what that wasted energy might have accomplished we cannot know. We do know it could have been put to more constructive uses.

The Red Scare grew in an atmosphere of crisis. Americans were not prepared for the vast and rapid social changes that followed World War II. That gigantic conflict was to have ushered in a safer, more democratic world. Certainly, progress had been made in Western Europe. But in Asia, it was a different story. China, the world's most populous nation, had fallen to the Communists in 1949; the French were having a tough time trying to reestablish control over Indochina. A nationalist-Communist, Ho Chi Minh (whose name means "he who enlightens" in Vietnamese), was leading a revolution for Vietnamese independence from France. Full-scale war had broken out there in 1946 and showed no signs of abating. The Soviet explosion of an atomic bomb in August 1949 soon sent tremors of fear across the previously impregnable United States.

Truman personally despised the opportunistic "Red hunters." It is only one of the countless ironies of the cold war that his own administration did much to raise the level of fear to hysteria. Truman had recognized that to gain popular support for peacetime programs such as the Marshall Plan, he would need to "scare hell" out of the American people. And that is precisely what the president and Dean Acheson did. If the American people weren't scared, so the administration's reasoning went, they wouldn't put up with the increased defense expenditures.

Fears were aroused by the so-called experts on

communism, such as J. Edgar Hoover, head of the Federal Bureau of Investigation. Hoover claimed in 1946 that "Red Fascism" had become a major force in unions, newspapers, magazines, book publishing, churches, and the motion picture industry, among others. (In fact, communism was a major force in none of these areas.) Reports of espionage and subversion by Communists in the United States were issued with extraordinary frequency in the late 1940s and the 1950s.

Not all reports were the product of overactive imaginations. In March 1945, the Office of Strategic Services, the predecessor to the CIA, raided the offices of an Asian-American magazine in Manhattan and discovered top-secret State Department documents in their files. The editor and several State Department employees were indicted, but the case fell apart when it was discovered that the OSS hadn't obtained a search warrant to enter the magazine's offices.

Later that same year, twenty-two people, some American, were arrested in Canada for passing secret documents to agents of the Soviet Union. The case appeared to prove beyond any doubt that a Soviet spy ring was alive and well in North America. In 1949, a Justice Department employee, Judith Coplon, was arrested by the FBI for passing documents to a Soviet agent.

Other espionage cases came to light in the late 1940s, each one lending a new degree of credence to outlandish claims of Communist subversion. No case received more attention than that which led to the imprisonment of a prominent former State Department employee with excellent credentials, Alger Hiss. Hiss, a

1929 Harvard Law School graduate, had won a clerkship with the renowned Supreme Court Justice Oliver Wendell Holmes and later served as undersecretary of state for the Far East.

This consummate New Dealer's career began to fall to pieces in the summer of 1948, when the House Un-American Activities Committee (HUAC) called a self-professed former Communist, Whittaker Chambers, as a witness. On August 3, Chambers, once a *Time* magazine editor, named Hiss as a one-time Communist agent with whom he had dealt directly in the late 1930s.

Hiss vehemently denied the charge two days later. But a freshman congressman from California, Richard Milhous Nixon, had been briefed on the Hiss case from a number of sources, and he was determined to prove Hiss a Communist. Under further questioning by Nixon (and others), Chambers appeared credible. The House Un-American Activities Committee then recalled Hiss, who now admitted that he had in fact known Chambers years ago, but he stuck to his claim that he had never been a Communist or helped the Communist cause. Hiss challenged Chambers to repeat his charges outside of Congress (Chambers was immune from slander charges as long as he leveled his accusations in Congressional testimony).

Chambers took up the challenge on the NBC show *Meet the Press*. He accused Hiss of having been a Communist; Hiss then promptly sued his accuser for slander.

Here the story begins to take on a bizarre quality. Chambers produced as evidence five microfilms of State Department documents he claimed he had received from Hiss, with some typed papers. It appeared that the documents had, at the very least, come from the government offices in which Hiss had served. Although the microfilms did not seem to show that the American Communists had received state secrets of vital importance, some of the material may have been useful to the Party, and that was enough for the government. Hiss was indicted on two counts of perjury (lying under oath) in December 1948; had the statute of limitations not run out, he would have been tried on espionage charges. The first Hiss trial resulted in a hung jury; at his second trial (January 1950), he was found guilty of perjury and sentenced to five years in prison.

Was Hiss, a man with a long record of government service, in fact guilty of espionage? Decades after the headlines have faded from public view, many students of this celebrated and controversial case believe Hiss was framed by the FBI. For many conservatives at the time, Hiss' guilt was beyond question. It only served to confirm their long-held suspicions that the "socialist" programs of the New Deal (government-run programs designed to heal the ailing U.S. economy in the 1930s) were supported and carried out by Communist sympathizers like Alger Hiss. Congressman Karl E. Mundt spoke for legions of such conservatives when he remarked that the nation "for years had been run by New Dealers, Fair Dealers, Misdealers and Hiss dealers who have shuttled back and forth between Freedom and Red Fascism like a pendulum on a KuKoo clock."[1]

Others held a different view, seeing the Hiss case as the opening act in a long and nasty play in which those whose ideas didn't fit the conservative mold were unfairly maligned in the name of national security. Harry Truman called the case a red herring (something that serves as a distraction from the central issues). He felt that Republican opportunists had pressed the charges to distract the public from the failures of the Republican Congress. Eleanor Roosevelt rushed to Hiss' defense, as did many liberal newspapers.

The public fascination with the Hiss case was kept alive by other events, the most prominent being the war in Korea. Soon after the outbreak of that conflict, a leftist engineer and longtime member of the Communist Party, Julius Rosenberg, was arrested by the FBI and accused of passing atomic secrets to Soviet agents. His wife, Ethel, was arrested for the same crime.

The charges against the Rosenbergs had arisen from the FBI's interrogation of Klaus Fuchs, a physicist whom a British court had already convicted of selling atomic secrets. Fuchs put the FBI onto a machinist-draftsman who had worked on the Manhattan Project, the top-secret U.S. government atomic bomb program. He was David Greenglass—Ethel Rosenberg's brother. Greenglass revealed that Julius had been the man to bring him into the Russian spy ring in the first place. The Rosenbergs were put on trial in New York for espionage, a federal offense. They were convicted and sentenced to death, and on June 19, 1953, the couple was executed in Sing Sing prison, in Ossining, New York. They were the only U.S. citizens ever executed on espionage charges.

The Rosenberg case caused a national furor and heightened fears that the country was in danger of being undermined from within. Many felt the couple had never been spies and that an elaborately planned FBI plot had been put in motion to frame them. (When the former Soviet Union began to release many of its secret files in the early 1990s, it became clear once and for all that the Rosenbergs had been working with the KGB, although the extent or impact of their spying isn't clear as of this writing.)

Long before either the Hiss case or the Rosenberg case came into public view, President Truman worried over the excessive fears of Communist subversion in the United States. He knew, as did other shrewd observers of American politics, that innuendos and accusations of radicalism were effective devices used by Republicans to discredit Democratic rivals, and vice versa. But he also recognized that the furor over Communists was eroding the people's faith in their government. Something had to be done to buttress the faith of doubters.

Thus in mid-1947, the federal loyalty program was born. All civilian employees in the executive branch were subject to extensive background checks carried out by review boards. If anything questionable was found lurking in a civilian employee's background, the person could be dismissed from government service. Dismissal could result even if the review boards found "reasonable grounds" simply for *believing* the employee's loyalty was questionable.

The determination of *which* groups were "subversive" was left entirely up to the judgment of the U.S. attorney general, who issued the first official list of subversive organizations in December 1947. No precise definition of loyalty was ever put forward by the government. Could one advocate, for instance, a change in race relations in the South and remain (officially) a loyal citizen? Was it disloyal to criticize the government's handling of a foreign-affairs crisis? The answers, under the law, were murky.

These vagaries were what made the federal loyalty program such a disaster, such an affront to the Bill of Rights, to the freedoms of speech and the press and the right of association, as well as to freedom of thought. "What was significant about the program," commented one observer,

> was that it was not designed to punish overt acts after they were committed. It was designed instead to make possible the ouster of a civil servant on the basis of a state of mind. The new premise of loyalty was that a spy might not be a figure of suspense fiction but an innocuous-looking bureaucrat. Moreover, since Communist spies had not done their work for foreign gold but in the service of an idea, it was possible that certain thoughts, attitudes, readings, and associations could prepare someone for spying, could become part of an intellectual journey that led down the road to treason.[2]

Not long after taking office in 1953, President Dwight D. Eisenhower established a new category of dismissable federal employee: the "security risk." Just who were these people? One could be classified as such for almost any reason: for drinking too much, for having something in one's family history that might pave the way to blackmail, for seeing a psychologist. During the Eisenhower years about fifteen hundred employees were dismissed as security risks. Six thousand additional civil servants left office, in large measure because of the peculiar stresses associated with government service during this anguished time of doubt and paranoia.

The crusade to stamp out Communist influence within the United States had an oppressive and stultifying impact on many aspects of life. It affected education, the entertainment industry, and the arts. Red hunting as a national pastime brought with it a movement to cleanse classrooms of books with "un-American" ideas. Teachers in many states were required to sign loyalty oaths; those with "subversive" notions were held up by school boards around the country as unfit to teach children.

The assault on beliefs was sometimes absurd: one woman in Indiana began a crusade to eliminate the story of Robin Hood from American classrooms—its message of robbing from the rich and giving to the poor seemed to her an attack on free enterprise and the "American way of life."

The FBI, under the stewardship of J. Edgar Hoover (surely one of the nation's most vigilant Red haters), undertook an overly zealous search for enemies of the state. College professors, particularly those who had shown some interest in communism during the 1930s (as many had at that time), were a preferred target. Spurred on by such conservative organizations as the American Legion and the Sons of the American

Revolution, state governments began to ferret out those colleges and universities that permitted the espousal of "radical" ideas.

Individual states set up their own boards of inquiry, often modeling these on the House Un-American Activities Committee. For example, the University of Washington lodged charges against six professors who had been investigated by a state committee examining the possibility of there being Communists in the state of Washington. Three of the professors were charged with concealing their membership in the Communist Party and were accused of professional incompetence. Two of the three admitted being Party members. The third denied ever having been a Communist.

The university committee that reviewed the cases found Communist Party membership to be insufficient cause for dismissal; it recommended to the state board of regents that only the man who denied membership be dismissed, for dishonesty. But the university president recommended that the admitted Communists be dismissed as well, on the ground that Communists lacked the capacity for independent thought that real scholarship required. All three were dismissed.

In Illinois, the Seditious Activities Investigating Commission undertook a search for Reds among the faculty at the prestigious University of Chicago. The chancellor of the university, Robert M. Hutchins, a man of unimpeachable integrity, stood firm and successfully defended his faculty against unwarranted accusations. The real danger to American institutions lay not in the few people of radical persuasion who didn't believe in those institutions, said Hutchins, but in the growing "miasma of thought control."[3]

While the state investigative committees vigorously pursued Communists within the universities, the federal government's activities accelerated. In 1947, HUAC began a highly publicized (and cynical) investigation of the film business. Movie people, like college professors, made easy targets, and they created publicity for the anti-Communist cause. Many of Hollywood's corps of screenwriters had strong left-wing credentials. In the 1930s, when the entire capitalist system was in the throes of the Great Depression, writers and artists of all kinds had joined the American Communist Party in droves. A few still belonged. Surely, HUAC members feared, these writers were busy inserting anti-American themes and ideas into their movies. HUAC members were deeply troubled, too, by Hollywood's lack of interest in what they considered "truly pro-American" films.

The hearings took on the coloration of a circus as the accusers stumbled from one question to another in their effort to unearth any sign of Red contamination in the movies. Some screenwriters refused to respond to questions concerning their political views, present or past. Ten—including Lester Cole and Dalton Trumbo, two of the most accomplished men in Hollywood—were cited for contempt of Congress and sentenced to prison terms. They became known as the Hollywood Ten.

Initially, studio executives had resisted the HUAC intrusions. But sensing the gravity of the charges and the potential impact of negative publicity, they soon caved in to congressional pressure and blacklisted the ten writers; that is, they denied the writers work in their chosen craft after leaving prison. "HUAC ran roughshod over Hollywood," observed Scott and Barbara Seigel, "because everyone in the industry was afraid of being labeled 'red' if they spoke out against the committee . . . [I]n the end more than one thousand people were smeared with the Communist label and found that they were unable to defend themselves. Many didn't even know they were on the blacklist until they suddenly couldn't find work."[4]

It was much the same in other walks of life. The number of teachers in the United States—or for that matter the number of scientists, municipal officials, clergy, or people serving in the State Department—who really opposed the legitimacy of the U.S. government or the principles on which it was based was exceedingly small. The tragedy of the "witch-hunts" was not only that so many innocent people were unjustly accused as it was that so many never escaped the shadows cast by their accusers in the first place.

By 1950, loyalty oaths (formal assertions of one's loyalty to the U.S. government), general fear and suspicion of one's neighbors and colleagues, purges in universities and labor unions—all of these hovered over the national scene like a huge black cloud.

Probably the most significant piece of anti-Communist legislation of this era was the McCarran Act, which was also known as the Internal Security Act of 1950. The McCarran Act created a Subversive Activities Control Board, which had the power to identify not only actual Communist organizations but those that were

"Communist-infiltrated" as well. In addition, the act gave the president the right to place suspect Communists in detention without a trial during times of national emergency. To his credit, President Truman vetoed the act; but support in Congress proved strong enough to override the veto, and the McCarran Act did indeed become law.

More trouble lay in the future, and much of it came in the form of a junior senator from the state of Wisconsin. At the turn of the new decade of the 1950s, Joseph R. McCarthy, a former state judge of middling quality and Marine Corps intelligence officer, was looking for an issue—any issue—that might propel him into the national limelight.

Truth be told, there weren't many in Washington who expected a great deal from Senator Joe McCarthy. This burly, sociable Republican's Senate record had been unremarkable. Elected to the Senate in 1946, he had no important legislation to his credit. He had a reputation as a fast talker and an opportunist. McCarthy had embellished his own history, even telling people around Washington that he'd seen combat as a tailgunner on a U.S. Marine bomber during World War II (in fact he never had). His detractors used to refer to him to him derisively as "Tailgunner Joe."

Senator McCarthy's journey from obscurity to prominence began on February 9, 1950. He was making a routine speech in Wheeling, West Virginia, and his message was clear enough: America was losing the cold war to the Communists. And Joe McCarthy knew why:

The reason why we find ourselves in a position of impotency is not because the enemy has sent men to invade our shores, but rather because of the traitorous actions of those . . . who have had all the benefits that the wealthiest nation has to offer—the finest homes, the finest college education, and the finest jobs in Government we can give.[5]

McCarthy went on to mention, in dramatic fashion, that in his hand he held a list of conspirators (some say he used the number 205, other sources say 57) who were betraying the very government they had sworn to serve. McCarthy couldn't have substantiated these charges— he had done almost no research on anybody on the list—but his speech caught the attention of newspaper editors all over the country, and within a few days, Joe McCarthy had the notoriety he had sought. The State Department issued several flat denials: There were no Communists within its ranks. On February 16, President Truman himself responded that "there was not a word of truth" in the accusations.[6]

Soon thereafter, a special Senate subcommittee under the chairmanship of Democrat Millard Tydings was assembled to investigate the accusations. The Wisconsin senator would have to answer to a committee of his colleagues, but his wish had come true: He was becoming famous. Within weeks, his name was inseparable from anticommunism and conspiracy.

Before the subcommittee, on March 8, the Wisconsin senator displayed a natural talent for obscuring the truth. He dodged and weaved around questions designed to clarify his evidence and responded to questions with even more attacks.

As time went on, the press put increasing pressure on McCarthy to produce solid evidence of conspiracy. Again in the Tydings committee hearings, McCarthy said he "would rise or fall" on the case of a "top Russian spy" in the State Department. The supposed spy was Owen Lattimore, an expert on China who had worked intermittently for State.

Lattimore ably defended himself against the espionage charges. He had, in fact, leaked some documents to a journal designed to discredit China's incompetent nationalist leader, Chiang Kai-shek. That might have been indiscreet, but it was not espionage. On March 30, McCarthy conceded that Lattimore was no spy, but he produced a witness who testified he had heard Communist Party members refer to Lattimore as a Communist. Lattimore again ably defended himself, but as would happen throughout the period of McCarthy's terror, the charges, not the truth, made headlines.

The accusation that struck home with the most force was too broad for anyone to defend against, namely, that as one of the architects of U.S. policy in the Far East, Lattimore had "sold out," or lost control of, all of mainland China to the Communists. The accusation had the unfortunate effect of discrediting all the China experts in the State Department, and the result was that for the next twenty years, the U.S. government was deprived of invaluable expert advice on matters Chinese.

Finally the Tydings committee issued its report on McCarthy's wild charges. It amounted to a scathing indictment of the senator: His claims were improperly researched, his methods unethical and slipshod. But the Republicans on the largely Democratic committee rose to defend the senator; they saw the report as a biased attempt to discredit their entire party.

McCarthy pressed on, undaunted by his critics. He accused even a great war hero, General George Catlett Marshall, of participating in a "great conspiracy" that had produced a series of setbacks for the United States in the cold war struggle. It was, McCarthy averred, "a conspiracy so immense as to dwarf any such venture in the history of man."[7]

This was it—the heart of McCarthy's appeal. Americans found it easy to believe there *was* a conspiracy. What else could explain the setbacks—the loss of the atomic bomb monopoly, China, Czechoslovakia—given the nation's unique power and virtue? The East Coast intellectuals, the foreign-policy establishment crowd, and the fancy-talking bankers, lawyers, and diplomats had let their country down, sold it out.

Joe McCarthy remained a potent and disruptive force throughout the early 1950s. By the time Eisenhower entered the White House, the Republican senator had become an acute embarrassment to his party and to the president. His outrageous charges against Eisenhower's choice for the ambassadorship to the Soviet Union, Charles E. Bohlen, proved particularly irritating. In 1953 alone, McCarthy led no less than ten public hearings to expose *current* espionage in government. He was, in effect, meddling in the president's conduct of foreign affairs.

Then, in early 1954, McCarthy overreached himself. He attacked the U.S. Army, claiming that it had knowingly drafted a "pink" dentist, Irving Peress, and that, once the army brass had learned McCarthy was "on to them," they had given Peress an honorable discharge. The president himself weighed in behind the Army; he began to show signs of his contempt for the demagogue from Wisconsin.

From April into June 1954, the Army-McCarthy hearings were broadcast live on television: The bullying, crass techniques of the leading figure of the witch-hunt era were put on national display. He behaved disgracefully, and he thoroughly discredited himself. At one point in the hearings, after McCarthy had leveled a series of unfounded charges of disloyalty, the army counsel, Joseph N. Welch, asked the critical question that, since that time, has been associated with Joe McCarthy's downfall: "At long last, sir, have you no sense of decency left? Have you no sense of decency?"[8]

Soon thereafter, the Senate began its own investigation of McCarthy. Finally, in December 1954, he was formally censured by his colleagues. His downfall complete, he died a broken alcoholic in 1957. By then the witch-hunts were all over, but the damage they had done to thousands of loyal Americans was not easily undone. A new term, *McCarthyism*—meaning a public official's use of the tactics of reckless accusation and implication of guilt by association—entered the American political lexicon.

The origins of McCarthyism were complex; its effects were both devastating and lasting. Long after Tailgunner

Joe was in his grave, anticommunism still maintained its hold on American life. It remained a powerful, omnipresent factor in politics. It affected the development of industry and the economy. It even appeared to alter the meaning of the word *American*—for by the mid-1950s, being a "good" American meant being hostile to Communist ideas and aspirations.

The crusade against communism was shaped by and reflected in popular culture in the United States. Nowhere was this more apparent than in television programming. In 1950, 3.1 million television sets had been bought by Americans. By 1955, there were 32 million sets in operation, and ten thousand Americans *a day* were purchasing their first set. As the 1950s went on, more and more people were entertaining themselves by watching programs on the screen in their living rooms, and a large number of these early TV series explored cold war themes and plots. Such programs as *Foreign Intrigue, Passport to Danger,* and *I Led Three Lives* popularized the simplistic idea that the struggle between East and West was a deadly serious—and easily understood—struggle between the forces of light and darkness.

Documentaries of the era, such as NBC's "Nightmare in Red," a history of the Soviet Union, tended to reinforce stereotypes rather than provide balanced, informative accounts. News programs, too, preferred patriotism and propaganda to objectivity and dispassionate inquiry. As one student of cold war culture has observed, "Rather than adapting a detached or independent position, which the First Amendment presumably permitted, television tended to vindicate a militaristic response to the Soviet challenge."[9]

Moviemakers, intimidated and enfeebled by the witch-hunts, were no more interested in challenging conventional wisdom on communism than were television executives. Scores of propagandistic anti-Communist films were distributed from the late 1940s through the early 1960s, from *The Red Menace* (1949) and *I Was a Communist for the FBI* (1951) to the low-budget *We'll Bury You!* (1962), a "documentary" about Soviet Russia.

It wasn't until the early 1960s that the film industry began to recapture its vitality and independence and to challenge cold war myths in a creative way. *The Spy Who Came in from the Cold,* published in 1963, was among the first thrillers to probe the complicated moral dilemmas and peculiar sacrifices of the East-West struggle.

Brooklyn-born director Stanley Kubrick's hilarious black comedy, *Dr. Strangelove* (1964), a big hit at the time of its release, milked rabid anticommunism for one laugh after another. In *Dr. Strangelove,* U.S. Air Force General Jack T. Ripper, fearing that "the Commies" have tampered with Americans' "precious bodily fluids" through the water fluoridation process, sends a wing of bomb-laden B-52 bombers into Russia on his own initiative. In the film, with World War III about to begin, U.S. President Murkin Muffley assembles his top advisers in the Pentagon "War Room." After high-ranking U.S. Air Force General Buck Turgidson explains that "recall" of the bombers isn't really an option—only the psychotic Ripper has the proper code and he cannot be reached—the general suggests that the *right* course of action under the "regrettable" circumstances would be to "launch an all-out nuclear attack." If the United States were to do so, the gung-ho Turgidson intones excitedly, "we'd stand a damn good chance of catching them [the Soviets] with their pants down!"

While many critics questioned whether a comedy about nuclear holocaust was in good taste, others saw it as a refreshing departure. The social philosopher Lewis Mumford wrote in the *New York Times* that "this film is the first break in the catatonic cold war trance that has so long held our country in its rigid grip."[10] *Dr. Strangelove* suggested that in the arena of cold war, it wasn't so easy to distinguish the good guys from the bad. In the complicated world of nuclear confrontation, people had a great deal more to fear than Soviet aggression. *Dr. Strangelove*'s popularity showed that more and more Americans were impatient with the pieties and stereotypes of the 1950s.

By the early 1960s, the anti-Communist consensus was beginning to break apart. More and more people were questioning the simplistic ideas about the East-West struggle in the movies and in life as well.

CHAPTER SIX

THE EISENHOWER YEARS

By mid-1952, containment, the basic American strategy for coping with world communism, had been in place for more than four years, and it was coming under attack. So was the Democratic Party, which had put the policy in place. A great many people both in the government and out found the policy wanting. The United States, after all, was the most powerful nation on earth; it had the most dynamic economy and a nuclear arsenal that dwarfed that of the Soviet Union, its chief rival. Why, it was asked with some impatience, was the country pursuing a defensive policy that left the initiative to the Communists? The sense of dissatisfaction was most acute regarding Korea, where Harry Truman's refusal to press forward to "liberate" North Korea from communism brought endless criticism from the press and the general public. Joe McCarthy's diatribes over the loss of China had touched a nerve among the public: It was not enough to be vigilant and wait patiently for communism to collapse from within. Containment needed to be scrapped or, at the very least, reinvigorated.

Dissatisfaction with containment was one of the ingredients that led to the November 1952 election of the World War II supreme commander of the Allied Expeditionary Forces in Western Europe, Republican Dwight David Eisenhower, to the U.S. presidency. There were other reasons. Ike's promise to go to Korea and end the war there had virtually guaranteed his election. He made good on the promise, but only after hinting to the Chinese that unless their intransigence at the negotiating table ceased, the United States would use nuclear weapons.

Then, too, there was Eisenhower's immense personal appeal, his unforgettable wide smile. He was a proven leader who had accomplished great things. It was he who had been responsible for the planning and successful execution of the D-day landing, the greatest amphibious operation in the history of warfare. He was unpretentious and strong willed and enjoyed a reputation for reasonableness. Some felt he was the only man in the West who could stand up to Stalin.

The Eisenhower years have been described as a time of complacency in American society. There is some truth in that. Ike embodied the easygoing temper of the times. He did not want to implement great change in a country that appeared, by almost any measure, to be prospering. His critics, some of them, felt he preferred to let the country run itself while he played golf. It was said during his presidency that the president from Kansas was impatient with details, although recent scholars have challenged this assessment. He avoided controversial causes and carefully guarded his immense public esteem. Wary of grand pronouncements, he liked to work behind the scenes. His vice-president, Richard M. Nixon, said it was characteristic of Eisenhower never to take direct action if he could achieve his objective from the sidelines.

Nevertheless, the 1950s were eventful years in the arena of international politics. It was during Ike's tenure that the rivalry between East and West, between communism and democratic capitalism, became a truly global affair. Indeed, the cold war cast its shadow everywhere: in the jungles of Southeast Asia, where Vietnam and Malaya were engaged in separate struggles that had strong cold war overtones; in the Middle East, where the Western countries were anxious about Russia's coveting the precious oil fields of Iraq and Iran; in South and Central America, where poverty and social injustice, often inflicted by corrupt regimes friendly to the West, lent credence to the ideas of leftist revolutionaries; and, of course, in a divided Europe.

It was in the 1950s that the United States engineered a number of alliances beyond Europe designed to deter Communist adventurism: the Southeast Asian Treaty Organization (SEATO), signed in 1954, and the Baghdad Pact in the Middle East, a 1955 alliance that the United States did not officially sign. Other treaties were signed with South Korea and Spain. Several potentially disastrous crises were thus defused before the superpowers resorted to military hostilities.

With the Eisenhower administration a new style of foreign policy emerged, as well as new, more assertive ideas about what the United States hoped to achieve in world affairs. The style was paradoxical, a peculiar mixture of the temperaments of the administration's two major foreign-policy figures. The president was known as a practical, easygoing man. His greatest skill as a politician was his ability to bring constructive compromise out of conflicting viewpoints.

Ike's secretary of state, John Foster Dulles, was as sober and upright as his Puritan forebears, and just as moralistic. He saw the struggle between communism and democracy in religious terms, a fight to the finish between good and evil. Dulles, the grandson of one secretary of state and the nephew of another, felt that, in the age of the cold war, neutrality was an "obsolete conception."[1] The Republican Party platform for 1952, written largely by Dulles, castigated the "negative, futile and immoral policy of 'containment' which abandons countless human beings to a despotism and godless terrorism."[2] The secretary of state spoke frequently about the "liberation" of the "enslaved" peoples of Eastern Europe, and for a while, early in the administration, leaders in the Western European countries thought the United States might be seeking a way to take on the Soviets directly, to win back freedom for the enslaved. John Foster Dulles talked a tough game. His tendency to see world politics as a struggle of good versus evil scared more practical-minded politicians. Winston Churchill, once reflecting on Dulles's penchant for crisis mongering, called the American secretary of state "a bull . . . who carries his own china closet with him."[3]

Ike respected Dulles's keen mind and dedication to the cause, although he was sometimes troubled by his secretary of state's moralizing and his distaste for negotiation with the Soviets. Once, not long after Stalin died in 1953, the State Department criticized the draft of a presidential speech as being too conciliatory. Ike responded, "If Mr. Dulles and all his sophisticated advisers really mean they can not talk peace seriously, then I am in the wrong pew."[4]

Nevertheless, it was Dulles who made the most visible pronouncements of the administration when it came to the Soviets. The key innovation in the Eisenhower administration's cold war strategy, dubbed the New Look, was called massive retaliation. It meant just what it said: The United States might respond to any future Soviet act of aggression with hydrogen bombs. Thus, the best course of action was for the United States (and its allies) to encourage the belief among the leaders of the Soviet Union that any offensive move on their part, no matter where, could trigger a devastating nuclear attack.

Massive retaliation had a number of appealing features. It offered the United States a deterrent policy that saved millions of defense dollars. Nuclear weapons were more destructive but also far less expensive than conventional forces, which had huge payrolls and supply bills, even in peacetime. The economic advantage of nuclear weapons over conventional ones appealed to Ike, who held that the temptation to spend recklessly on defense must be strongly checked. The president was most anxious to reduce American expenditures on defense (Truman's defense budgets had exceeded $50 billion), and massive retaliation would provide the justification for those reductions.

The Democratic Party critics of massive retaliation in Congress didn't quarrel with the notion of saving money. Their concerns rested with the practical defects of the idea. What if a Soviet proxy, a Communist state that would do Moscow's bidding, started a brushfire war in one of the developing nations? What good were nuclear weapons in the struggle against active Communist guerrilla movements in peasant societies? Massive retaliation, in other words, placed great limits on how and where the military could respond in a crisis. It was unwise to swat flies with sledgehammers. The Eisenhower administration, throughout its tenure, downplayed these awkward questions, despite the fact that they dealt with very real problems.

As it happened, these somewhat hawkish cold war policies were counterbalanced by President Eisenhower's deep conservatism and his determination, perhaps above all else, to keep the world free from the horrors of a nuclear exchange. Eisenhower had an abiding hatred of the Communist system. He had always felt the United States needed to deal with the Soviets from a position of strength. Yet throughout his eight years in office, he showed great restraint when it came to taking military action. He never imagined that victory in the cold war would come about by direct military confrontation. He hoped that peaceful diplomacy and the economic success of Western capitalism would bring about reform in Soviet behavior.

Soon after the new administration took up residence in the White House, two developments occurred that were to have resounding effects on the future of the cold war. The first was the death of Joseph Stalin in March 1953, which left a vacuum in the mysterious world of Soviet power politics.

The second was more ominous. In August 1953, less than a year after the United States had acquired the hydrogen bomb (and thereby a considerable edge in the arms race), Georgy Malenkov, one of several key Soviet political leaders, announced that the USSR had exploded a similar weapon. The American monopoly on the hydrogen bomb, vastly more powerful than the atomic bombs dropped during World War II, had evaporated far more quickly than anyone in Washington had predicted. (Britain had also developed its own H-bomb, in 1952.)

It was an event that made thoughts about the world going up in smoke frighteningly real. The initial reaction on the part of John Foster Dulles was one of outright disbelief—he thought it was a ruse. But it turned out to be the truth, and the defense experts and scientists at the Pentagon were put to work preparing reports for the new administration concerning the length of time it would take the Soviets to develop a reliable method of delivering the bomb to the United States, and what might be done to counter that development. They were important issues: Strategists reasoned that the major deterrent to a Soviet attack on Europe was the American capacity to strike at the heart of the Soviet Union with H-bombs without fear of retaliation. Now things must be entirely rethought. And not just by strategists, but by statesmen and the citizens they represented all over the world. The presence of the H-bomb in the arsenals of the Americans and now in those of the Soviet Union had far-reaching effects for everyone. As Winston Churchill eloquently pointed out in 1955:

> The entire foundation of human affairs was revolutionized and mankind placed in a situation both measureless and laden with doom. . . . It may well be that we shall, by a process of sublime irony, have reached a stage in history where safety will be the sturdy child of terror, and survival the twin brother of annihilation.[5]

Perhaps there was a ray of hope amid the general gloom that pervaded Washington when it was learned that the Russians had the hydrogen bomb. For one thing, Stalin's successors, Georgy Malenkov (soon to nearly vanish from the scene) and the politically astute Nikita Khrushchev, displayed an inclination to reduce tensions. Kremlin proclamations now de-emphasized the importance of exporting revolution, and cuts were made in expenditures in the industries that kept the Soviet Union's huge armed forces at the ready. There were even subtle indications that the new leaders might open up the very closed political institutions of the USSR, exposing their mysterious workings to the outside world.

The initial problem for Ike and his advisers was to determine just what these unexpected changes in Soviet attitude actually meant. Was the Kremlin merely taking a softer approach in the hope of winning support from the Europeans, thereby driving a wedge into the Atlantic alliance? Or were the two Soviet leaders coming to the welcome conclusion that their own interests would be better served by taking a less hostile view of Western intentions?

The president's initial responses to the Soviets were couched in positive terms. The United States would welcome an improved relationship. But Eisenhower wanted concrete proof that the Russians were prepared to curtail their mischief-making around the world. If the Soviets sought détente (a lessening of tension), they should call off their proxies in Malaya and Indochina and allow free elections in North Korea. Ike called for Soviet concessions on Austria, which remained in diplomatic limbo: No peace treaty had been signed despite years of negotiations among the victors of World War II.

The U.S. president was saying, as historian Walter LaFeber put it, that "a multitude of questions all [needed to] be solved at once."[6] Ike's position made the European allies, particularly the British, uneasy. They preferred to tackle one issue at a time.

Washington remained wary, which caused serious friction among the allies. They worried that the United States was being too cautious by not taking advantage of the possible changes in the Soviet Union now that Stalin was in his grave.

Then in mid-June 1953 came an event that seemed to shut the door on the possibility of some sort of East-West rapprochement: The East German government refused to repeal its 1952 rules requiring workers to produce more without an increase in pay. A full-scale strike broke out in East Berlin. The East Germans tore down Soviet flags and marched in the streets for political freedom. Strikes and riots spread to other East German cities. The United States government issued statements applauding the strikes, urging the laborers forward.

Soviet tanks moved in to stop the demonstrators. The strikers looked for further signs of U.S. support, but none were forthcoming. Verbal support was as far as the cautious Eisenhower was prepared to go. He would not throw American troops into a cause that, however morally correct, was in the Soviet sphere of influence. The East German uprising was crushed. Liberation of the "enslaved peoples" of Eastern Europe, as John Foster Dulles called them, evidently would have to wait.

Other crises with implications for the world balance of power soon materialized. The first of these was in Iran, whose ruler, the shah, enjoyed strong support from the United States. Here the problem was not anything so tangible as Russian atomic weapons or troops but the possibility that the USSR could exploit Iranian nationalism for its own ends.

The situation in Iran was this: In 1951 Mohammad Mosaddeq, the Iranian premier, led a popular movement to have the Iranian government take over the Anglo-Iranian oil company, which was owned by Britain. When the British demanded compensation for the seizure during the same year, the Iranians refused. They didn't have the funds and resented the British, who had provided the technical expertise to extract the oil and who then reaped most of the profits.

A boycott of Iran by the Western powers put considerable pressure on the Iranian government, for oil sales provided more than one-quarter of Iran's total income. John Foster Dulles felt the crisis opened the door for Communist subversion in Iran. There were, in fact, persistent rumors of a large Soviet loan to Mosaddeq. The Soviets had long been looking to extend their influence in the Middle East. Given the importance of oil to the West, Dulles believed the United States had to act—and fast.

Not wanting to incite the wrath of Iran by siding openly with the British, the secretary of state attempted to broker a compromise. But, having failed to come to an agreement through diplomacy, he employed what would become a favored tactic of the cold war: using the CIA to funnel millions of U.S. dollars into the hands of friends (in this case the shah). It was a plan devised by the secretary's brother, CIA Director Allen Dulles, to eliminate Mosaddeq, who had been voted dictatorial powers by the Iranian parliament. After fighting between the pro- and anti-Mosaddeq factions, this plan succeeded in August 1953. Shah Mohammad Reza Pahlavi returned from a very brief exile, and Mosaddeq was jailed. Oil production resumed, with profits divided among a consortium of U.S., British, and Dutch companies and the Iranian government.

The resolution of the Iranian crisis was cause for celebration in Washington. Ike and Dulles knew that Stalin had long sought some sort of leverage over the oil fields, and with a pro-Western regime in Iran, they had frustrated Soviet desires.

Iran represented one of the early successes of the

Central Intelligence Agency's covert, or secret, programs. Ike relied on the CIA with increasing regularity to combat leftist revolutionaries who challenged pro-America regimes, particularly in Latin America. Today, in the post-Vietnam War era, the drawbacks of having a democracy use its intelligence forces in this manner have become painfully apparent. In the 1950s, however, the Washington foreign-policy establishment viewed such measures as fighting fire with fire. Psychological warfare, covert operations, and terrorism were pillars that upheld Communist states, whether in the Soviet Union, China, or Eastern Europe; and the West regularly employed some of the Communists' less savory tactics, too.

Just how effective the CIA could be as a tool for checking radicalism in Latin America was made clear in the spring of 1953 in Guatemala. That poor nation, roughly the size of the state of Tennessee, found itself embroiled in political turmoil, torn between conservatives, who wanted to preserve their privileged lifestyle, and leftists, many of whom were poor peasants and middle-class citizens fed up with social injustice. The reformers, led by President Jacobo Arbenz Guzmán, carried out a number of changes that the conservatives did not like but could live with. He confiscated more than 170,000 acres of land of the United Fruit Company, which was owned by Americans, and began to receive arms from the Eastern bloc. Ike gave the go-ahead for a CIA-sponsored coup. The agency trained and equipped Guatemalan exiles in Honduras, under the command of Guatemalan Carlos Castillo Armas. In June, this small force attacked Guatemala and soundly defeated forces loyal to Arbenz.

Once again the CIA had come through for the administration. Critics, however, felt that Eisenhower had been shortsighted. Only a small cadre of Communists were active in Guatemala, and Armas turned out to be anything but a progressive leader. Three years later he was assassinated. Many students of Latin American relations in the cold war era see the Guatemalan intervention as an example of an enduring and regrettable tendency on the part of the United States to assume that the voices of reform in Latin America arose not out of legitimate concerns for social justice, but out of the duplicities of Communists in Moscow.

In the spring of 1954 the Eisenhower administration faced a challenge with far more bearing on the power struggle between East and West than the storm in Guatemala. This time it was in French Indochina, in the ancient country of Vietnam. Much of the work carried out in the summer of 1954 in the Geneva Conference, attended by the leaders of the major (and some minor) powers, concerned the far-away region of Indochina. There the potent forces of nationalism, communism, colonialism, and damaged French pride converged.

No U.S. troops had set foot in this region, which lies to the southeast of China and stretches out like an open hand into the South China Sea. But the United States had a profound interest in what happened there, because U.S. money and moral support had played a critical role in the French Indochina War (1946–54).

That conflict pitted the forces of the popular nationalist-Communist leader, Ho Chi Minh, against French troops, including France's Foreign Legion. Ho wanted a united, independent Vietnam. The French were willing to grant limited independence to the Vietnamese, which to most of that nation's people meant no independence at all.

American aid to the French commenced in 1950. The Americans had been worried that the fall of China to communism was only the first of a series of setbacks in Asia, and although not anxious to appear to be supporting old colonial powers, the United States was soon paying the lion's share of the bill for fighting communism in Southeast Asia. Between 1950 and 1954, more than $1 billion in U.S. aid went to the French war effort, and a handful of American technicians and military advisers were sent in to help as well.

Despite France's technological superiority over the Vietminh (the Communist forces led by Ho Chi Minh), its war effort foundered. Like so many other peoples in the developing world, the Vietnamese detested the presence of their colonial masters. But France, whose pride had been greatly wounded by its quick defeat early in World War II at the hands of Germany, was determined to hold on to its colony. In March 1954, French troops fortified the remote village of Dien Bien Phu, hoping to draw the Vietnamese forces into a full-scale, conventional battle—something the lightly armed Vietminh had studiously avoided. But the plan backfired. Thousands of Vietnamese porters dragged Chinese-supplied artillery pieces hundreds of miles into the jungle *on foot*, surrounded the French, and proceeded to pound Dien Bien Phu to bits. Meanwhile, Vietminh infantry, in displays of remarkable tenacity and courage, assaulted and eliminated one French position after another.

Realizing that the end of Dien Bien Phu meant the end of the war, the French pleaded for direct U.S. intervention. For several weeks, the Eisenhower administration pondered the question. U.S. Air Force Chief of Staff Nathan Twining believed a few well-placed tactical (that is, battlefield) nuclear weapons would save the day. But Ike rejected the general's plan. After consulting with the British, he decided that the risks of involvement in another Asian war were too great.

The French garrison fell in May, and so ended the French Indochina War.

Ike's decision highlighted the great weakness of threatening Communists with nuclear bombs. Such a threat wasn't believable. The United States was not about to drop these awesome weapons on every Communist who decided to make trouble.

How, then, would the situation in Vietnam be resolved? Even before the fall of Dien Bien Phu, statesmen from nineteen nations had gathered in Geneva, Switzerland, in April 1954 for a great diplomatic conference to sort out matters on the Vietnam question and others. They hoped, among other things, to resolve the problems in Korea (the 1953 truce had been meant to be temporary) and to deal with the always-sensitive issue of a divided Germany. Little progress was made on either of those questions. As for Vietnam, a compromise was reached: Ho Chi Minh would govern the northern half of the country above the seventeenth parallel, and a pro-Western republic under Ba Dai was established in the south. Nationwide elections were scheduled for 1956 in Vietnam to bring about its reunification. The Russians had exerted pressure on the Vietnamese to accept the agreement, in hopes of gaining better relations with the French, who, like the Russians, were nervous about the Germans.

Within a year of the Geneva Conference (July 21, 1954), American aid was pouring into South Vietnam. American General J. Lawton Collins was put in charge of a military advisory group sent to train the South Vietnamese army to fend off the Communist army to the north. The United States' long and tragic involvement in Vietnam was well under way.

The collapse of the French in Indochina, the settlement at Geneva, the presence of a powerful and popular Communist regime in North Vietnam—all these developments unsettled Washington. John Foster Dulles, ever vigilant, began the push to establish a new anti-Communist alliance in Asia. The alliance, the Southeast Asian Treaty Organization (SEATO), was signed in Manila on September 8, 1954. It called upon the signatories to consult with one another should any government be threatened by either direct aggression or internal subversion. If the nation under such assault approved, the signatories could intervene on its behalf.

It was also agreed that an attack on a number of countries that had not joined the pact—South Vietnam, Cambodia, or Laos, for example—would be considered a threat to the "peace and safety" of the region. The

United States, Britain, France, Australia, New Zealand, Pakistan, the Philippines, and Thailand were parties to the agreement.

SEATO had the effect of expanding the United States' already large commitments to combat communism. It was one of numerous alliances, some with individual countries and some with regional groups, engineered by an administration that believed no place on earth was exempt from exploitation by leftist revolutionaries. SEATO lacked the teeth of NATO, because no party was *bound* to respond in the event of aggression. To many leaders of the developing nations, however, the whole arrangement seemed a perfect example of the American effort to dominate and exploit the weaker, poorer nations of the world. That they should have felt this was no mystery, for while the United States was not seeking outright political control of Southeast Asia, SEATO was obviously a way of tying the member nations closer to the United States and its capitalistic economic system.

For their part, the Eisenhower people defended the treaty as a necessary deterrent to Soviet ambition. By 1956, Khrushchev had put into place a subtle foreign policy that was in many ways more ambitious than Stalin's. In May 1955, in response to the formation of NATO, the Soviet Union announced the formation of its own great alliance: the Warsaw Pact, an organization of political and military cooperation among the USSR, Poland, Bulgaria, Albania, Hungary, East Germany, and Czechoslovakia. He courted third world nations with economic and military aid and undertook a vigorous public relations campaign designed to convince nations in Asia, Africa, and the Middle East that communism was the wave of the future. He also sought to improve relations with other Communist states, notably the People's Republic of China and Yugoslavia. By the end of that year, no fewer than fourteen Soviet economic and military assistance agreements had been signed with nations in the Middle East and Asia alone. (The Americans had similar arrangements with many more nations than the Soviets did; still, U.S. administrations continued to see Soviet alliances as provocative and essentially offensive in nature.)

In the midst of all this alliance building that began in Geneva in 1954 came a promising development: The Russians once again toned down their anti-Western rhetoric and in the spring of 1955 showed signs of a genuine desire to improve relations with the United States and its allies. A summit—the first superpower meeting since World War II had ended—was arranged for May in Geneva. Leaders of the United States, Britain, France, and the Soviet Union attended. Little of substance was resolved there. Eisenhower and Khrushchev met, and their personal relationship was cordial and respectful. Both leaders recognized the importance of appearing to the world as reasonable and responsible men, and the press spoke about a new "spirit of Geneva." This was the first of a number of cold war summits aimed at reducing tension and reaching a more constructive understanding.

The spirit of Geneva soon faced a tough test in the Middle East. General Gamal Abdel Nasser, the charismatic leader of Egypt, needed money if his poor, developing nation was to become economically self-sufficient. He was struggling against a hostile neighbor in Israel, which had recently humiliated Egypt by staging a successful military raid on the Gaza Strip (land Egypt had seized in 1948 from part of the area the UN had designated for a Palestinian state), so he also needed arms. He made inquiries in Washington, but the United States had no interest in escalating the arms race in so volatile a region. The Soviets, long frustrated in their efforts to obtain Middle Eastern friends, were more than happy to oblige. In August Nasser signed a military assistance agreement with the Soviet Union, and in September came an arms deal with the Czechs, who were noted for producing wonderfully effective small arms.

These developments troubled Washington and its allies, all of whom shared an interest in checking the burgeoning relationship between the Communist superpower and Egypt, a large, influential Middle Eastern state. As it happened, there were opportunities to do just that.

Nasser envisaged building a giant dam to harness the Nile River. Such a project could provide electric power and water to areas otherwise unsuitable for agriculture. John Foster Dulles was intensely interested. He cobbled together a deal; a loan of more than $50 million would come from the United States. Britain and the World Bank, one of the great Western lending institutions, would contribute as well. In return, the United States asked Nasser to resolve his ongoing dispute with Israel.

As 1956 began, it looked as though the deal for the huge dam might go through. Then things began to fall apart fast. Dulles encountered resistance from other members of Eisenhower's administration. Many in Washington found the loan too large, given that Nasser was an unpredictable entity who had received weapons from the East. Nasser didn't help matters when in May he announced an agreement for Poland to supply Egypt with weapons. Next, Nasser extended diplomatic relations to Communist China. Dulles was furious. On July 19, the Egyptian leader was told that the deal, which he had officially accepted two days earlier, was off.

Then came the shocker: On July 26, 1956, Nasser nationalized the Suez Canal Company. He claimed that the tolls collected from ships using the canal would be used to build the dam. Egyptian troops took over the strategically vital waterway, the shortest shipping lane between the Gulf of Suez and the Mediterranean Sea. Britain and France, who ran (and, in effect, owned) the Suez Canal, were dependent on Persian Gulf oil that came through the canal. They were not pleased. Anthony Eden, the British prime minister, summarized the problem in a single sentence: "The Egyptian has his thumb on our windpipe."[7]

In the late summer of 1956, Secretary of State Dulles made strenuous efforts to negotiate a settlement to the crisis. Unfortunately, the secretary of state's moralizing didn't sit well with any of the parties. While the talking continued, the British and the French conspired with the Israelis, whose southern port was being blockaded by Egypt. They planned to wrest control of the canal from the Egyptians by armed force.

As autumn approached and the plans for the Suez

invasion moved forward, a new crisis of great international import was already unfolding. Earlier that year, Khrushchev had begun to denounce the harsh policies of Stalin, who had died in 1953. In October 1956, an important Polish political prisoner, Wladislaw Gomulka, was released. Soon reform was in the air everywhere in Communist Poland. The contagion spread to Hungary, where the call went out from Communist intellectuals for reform and the reinstatement of the former elected Communist leader of that nation, Imre Nagy. The Hungarian secret police tried to crush the demonstrations, but their actions only led to more passionate outcries for freedom and reform.

In an unusual display of flexibility, the Kremlin agreed to allow Nagy to return to power on October 24. The act added fuel to the fire. The Hungarians now wanted even more: they called for the removal of all Soviet forces from Hungarian territory. Would the vise-like grip of the Soviets be relaxed? The world waited.

Then, on October 29, Washington's focus shifted back to the Middle East: Israeli troops attacked Egyptian forces in Egypt and took control of the Sinai peninsula. Two days later, British and French aircraft and naval forces joined the fight, attacking the surprised Egyptians.

Khrushchev now saw an opening. The surprise attacks by the "imperialists" would distract the world from events in Eastern Europe, where on October 30, Soviet troops had withdrawn from the Hungarian capital of Budapest and Premier Nagy had promised free elections and an end to the dictatorship. On

November 4, with the world's attention focused on the Middle East, Khrushchev sent Soviet armored troops back into Budapest. Over the course of about seven days, some thirty thousand Hungarians died trying to stop Soviet tanks with World War II–vintage rifles, pistols, and Molotov cocktail bombs. Almost simultaneously, the Soviet leader threatened to send Soviet "volunteers" into the Middle East imbroglio if the Anglo-French invasion was not halted.

In Washington and around the world, a new war scare broke out. The president put U.S. forces on worldwide alert and remarked to one of his close advisers that "if those fellows start something, we may have to hit 'em—and, if necessary, with everything in the bucket."[8] The United States put forward resolutions condemning the British, the French, and the Russians, all of whom, the Eisenhower administration believed, had acted with utter disregard for international law. By November 5, the French and the British began landing paratroopers to gain complete control of the Suez Canal and so appeared reluctant to halt their advance. Ike threatened to cut off their supply of much-needed American oil. The threat worked. On November 6—the day Eisenhower was reelected in a landslide victory over Democratic candidate Adlai E. Stevenson—a cease-fire was reached, and the Suez crisis was, at long last, defused.

What had these two situations meant in terms of international affairs and the direction of the cold war? For the Americans, some solace could be found in what did not happen. The Kremlin's effort to place the Soviet

Union squarely in the center of Middle Eastern affairs had been foiled. Suez also had the effect of finishing off illusions in Paris and London that France and Britain would continue to play crucial roles in the Middle East. As one observer put it, these two European nations

> entered the affair as colonial giants and emerged from it as faintly disreputable second-raters. It was now America's turn; the United States was suddenly the superpower arbiter in the Middle East. After Suez, almost by default, the United States assumed . . . the preeminent position it occupies in the Middle East today [1987].[9]

And what of the Hungarian rebellion? It reaffirmed the utter brutality of the Soviet regime in dealing with those in its orbit who sought to reassert independence. The appearance of Soviet tanks certainly crushed whatever had been left of the "spirit of Geneva," and it revealed, at least to the Eisenhower administration, that there was something of Stalin's hard-line attitude in Khrushchev.

Eisenhower's second term in office (1957–61) was marked by fewer crises but by a number of developments of lasting significance. In March 1957, Congress granted power to the president to extend financial and military assistance to any Middle Eastern country that requested it. This was part of the so-called Eisenhower Doctrine, which also gave Ike (and his successors) the right to assist any Middle Eastern country suffering under "armed aggression." The work of improving and expanding nuclear arsenals continued. It was now an article of faith in both Washington and Moscow that a critical ingredient in preserving the peace was the maintenance of a stabilizing balance in their nuclear arsenals. Meanwhile, the United States was building a huge fleet of long-range jet bombers to deliver nuclear weapons over thousands of miles.

In 1956 and 1957, the engineers and scientists of the superpowers grappled with the problems of developing the intercontinental ballistic missile (ICBM). These were rockets of enormous power, capable of projecting a nuclear warhead more than five thousand miles at a targeted military site or civilian population center. The first American ICBM was called the Atlas, and most defense watchers believed that it would be operational long before the Soviet ICBM would be. U.S. technology, after all, had long been the most sophisticated in the world, and the prosperity of the 1950s had instilled a sense of great confidence in American know-how.

Then came *Sputnik*. On October 4, 1957, the Soviet Union successfully launched the first satellite into space. The news was greeted in the United States with alarm bordering on panic. On December 6, the United States' answer to *Sputnik*, the *Vanguard* satellite, was scheduled for launch. When the moment of truth came, however, the rocket exploded on the launching pad. It was a humiliating moment for Washington and for American science.

The Russians, it seemed, were ahead of the United States, and ahead in an area of immense import.

Rockets that could launch satellites could easily launch nuclear warheads. Suddenly, American complacency was shaken; the cold war was now casting its shadow on American education. Did our kids know enough science and math? Were they falling behind their Soviet counterparts? The cry went up for increased spending on science education, lest the United States fall behind in the "space race." From the late 1950s onward, the space race became a highly visible part of the superpower rivalry.

In May of 1958, rocketry took a back seat to yet another Middle Eastern problem with cold war overtones. This time it was in Lebanon. Camille Chamoun, the pro-American leader of this small nation, claimed Communists were inspiring unrest, threatening the stability of his government and his people. Eisenhower dispatched naval forces to the area as a sign of support.

In nearby Iraq, admirers of Nasser assassinated King Faisal. The assassins, Iraqi army officers, hoped that the newly installed General Abdul Karim Kassem would turn from the West and remove Iraq from the Baghdad Pact, an alliance orchestrated by Dulles which had bound a number of Middle Eastern countries together to resist the spread of Communist influence. What would happen next? Both King Hussein of Jordan and President Chamoun of Lebanon felt their nations were in danger, on the verge of rebellion, chaos, and invasion from Egypt and neighboring Syria, both of which were receiving weapons and training from the Soviet Union.

Fourteen thousand U.S. troops, mostly marines, were put ashore in Lebanon. Elements of the United States Strategic Air Command—the military organization that controls the airplanes used in nuclear war—were deployed to the area as a warning to the Soviets not to take advantage of the turbulence. Order was restored, and the last American troops withdrew in October 1958.

In retrospect, it isn't clear that the Soviets or their allies were planning mischief in Lebanon. In a sense it didn't matter, since the United States had a strong interest in keeping Middle Eastern oil flowing out of the region in a predictable fashion.

Meanwhile, Premier Khrushchev was a busy man, determined to extend Soviet influence and prestige wherever possible. He often spoke of "peaceful coexistence" with the West and talked up the Communist system as a viable and attractive alternative model for the world's developing nations. Frustrated by the West's repeated successes at keeping his country out of the Middle East, he focused on matters closer to home.

On November 10, 1958, Khrushchev, under pressure for some sort of cold war victory, announced his displeasure over the continued Western presence in the city of Berlin. Unless some accommodation could be reached, he planned to turn over control of the city to the East Germans. It escaped no one's notice that the East Germans would be under no obligation to respect the access agreements and guarantees made with the Soviets regarding the division of Berlin at Yalta and Potsdam.

The Western powers, however, were not about to acquiesce, for Berlin was a city of immense symbolic and practical significance in the East-West rivalry. Months went by, and the Soviets did nothing. Berlin was very

TOP: Churchill, an ailing Roosevelt, and Stalin meet at Yalta in February 1945. During the controversial conference, the "Big Three" agreed to divide Germany into four sectors (Bettmann Archive).

CENTER: This is the mushroom cloud that hovered over Nagasaki, Japan, on August 8, 1945. The cold war came into being with the birth of the atomic age (National Archives).

BOTTOM: Harry S Truman, U.S. president, 1945-53 (National Archives).

The 1948 blockade of Berlin, isolated in the Soviet sector of Germany, help polarize Western and Communist attitudes. Here German children wave to a U.S. military plane airlifting supplies into Berlin to break the blockade (UPI/Bettmann).

The cold war turned hot with the conflict in Korea, 1950-53. Here U.S. Marines guard North Korean prisoners (National Archives).

War-Maker

47. Mao Tse-tung is the leader of the Chinese Reds who attacked the United Nations forces in Korea. His army was built up, in the first place, with the help of outlaws. Later the Russian Reds supplied him with arms and advisers. He captured the China mainland in three years of savage warfare against the Nationalist government. Mao delights in war. History, he says, "is written in blood and iron." The free world must find a way to keep war-makers like Mao Tse-tung from shedding the blood of innocent people.

FIGHT THE RED MENACE

© 1951 Bowman Gum, Inc., Phila., Pa., U.S.A.

ABOVE: In the early 1950s, no one in America was thought too young to "fight the Red menace" as this 1951 trading card attests (author's collection).

COMMUNIST PARTY ORGANIZATION U.S.A – FEB. 9, 1950

As the chairman of the Special Permanent Senate Subcommittee on Investigations, Senator Joseph McCarthy (at chart) rose to national prominence by denouncing suspected Communist infiltrators (UPI/Bettmann).

TOP: A freedom fighter burns a photo of Lenin during the Hungarian uprising of 1956 (UPI/Bettmann).

BOTTOM LEFT: The launching of the first space satellite, *Sputnik*, by the Russians on October 4, 1957, frightened Americans into a flat-out space race (UPI/Bettmann).

BOTTOM RIGHT: In the late 1950s, American president Dwight Eisenhower and Soviet premier Nikita Khrushchev preserved a fragile peace (UPI/Bettmann).

TOP: A U.S. intelligence photo, circa 1962, reveals the presence of Russian surface-to-air missiles in Cuba, just ninety miles off the Florida coast (U.S. Army Military History Institute).
BOTTOM: President John F. Kennedy faces the press during the Cuban Missile Crisis of October 1962. The whole world feared this incident would be the catalyst for nuclear war (UPI/Bettmann).

TOP: The cold war heated up again in Vietnam. Although the U.S. never officially declared war, from 1961 to 1975 over eight million Americans, such as this infantryman, served in Vietnam (U.S. Army Military History Institute).
BOTTOM LEFT: Mao Zedong, chairman of the Communist party, People's Republic of China, 1949-76 (Library of Congress).
BOTTOM CENTER: Ho Chi Minh, president of the Communist People's Republic of Vietnam, 1954-69 (National Archives).
BOTTOM RIGHT: Lyndon B. Johnson, U.S. president, 1963–69 (Department of Defense Still Media Records Center).

TOP: In February 1972, Richard Nixon became the first American president to visit Communist China. Here Nixon toasts the Chinese premier, Zhou Enlai (UPI/Bettmann).

CENTER LEFT: In 1974, President Gerald Ford met with Soviet Communist Party chief Leonid Brezhnev in Vladivostok, USSR (UPI/Bettmann).

CENTER RIGHT: During the 1980s, President Ronald Reagan and General Secretary of the Communist Party Mikhail Gorbachev's warm personal relationship resulted in unprecedented cooperation between the U.S. and the USSR (Reuters/Bettmann).

BOTTOM: U.S. president George Bush applauds Soviet president Mikhail Gorbachev in May 1990 (Reuters/Bettmann).

TOP: In anticipation of German reunification, young Berliners took picks and shovels to the Berlin Wall in November 1989 (Reuters/Bettmann).

CENTER: For the first time in nearly fifty years, East and West Berliners meet at Potsdamer Platz, where the Berlin Wall was torn down to make way for a new border crossing (Reuters/Bettmann).

BOTTOM: A Lithuanian woman protests an order from Moscow to evict Lithuanian appointees from the general prosecutor's office in Vilnius on April 5, 1990 (Reuters/Bettmann).

much in mind when the two superpower leaders met again, this time in Washington, in September 1959. But no decision was reached on the question, and Khrushchev said he had never issued an ultimatum to the West to leave Berlin or face unspecified consequences. The two men agreed to take up the question again the following spring at another summit meeting to be held in Paris.

For a brief time, the focus on foreign affairs and the cold war receded in the United States. Americans, both in and out of government, were preoccupied with the upcoming fall 1960 presidential election. John Foster Dulles, the tireless spokesman of American anticommunism, died in April, the victim of cancer. In May, a menacing-looking plane took off from a secret location in Pakistan and headed for the Soviet Union's airspace. Flights like this had been taking place regularly since 1956. The plane, built by the Lockheed Corporation of California, was called the U-2. It was an extraordinary airplane, capable of flying more than sixty thousand feet above the earth, out of range of most weapons. Like all other U-2s, it was equipped with a camera that could photograph the land below in great detail.

The May 1, 1960, flight was destined to change history: Somewhere near the city of Sverdlovsk, it was shot down by a Soviet rocket, and the pilot, Francis Gary Powers of the CIA, was captured. The Russians decided not to tell the United States about it, opting instead to put the mishap to good use. Khrushchev had in mind a humiliating scheme, and the Americans fell right into his trap.

It worked this way: Moscow announced to the world that U.S. airplanes had been detected inside Soviet airspace and demanded an explanation. Ike was in a sticky position. He had no plane, no pilot, and no knowledge of what Khrushchev knew. Seeking to keep the explosive news under the rug—that the United States was actively and regularly collecting intelligence information by flying its reconnaissance planes over Soviet territory—the CIA instructed the National Aeronautics and Space Administration (NASA) to issue a fabricated explanation: One of their high-flying weather reconnaissance planes had somehow come to a bad end. It was all perfectly innocent. . . .

On May 6, the Soviet premier let the other shoe drop: Not only did the Soviets have the pilot in hand, but they could prove that Powers had been engaged in something more than weather reconnaissance. The reaction in Washington and around the country was one of profound dismay. President Eisenhower took responsibility for the disaster, claiming that excessive Soviet secrecy had made the flights necessary to alert the United States to surprise nuclear attack.

The newspapers wrote of a runaway spy service that had bungled, once again. A few days later in Paris, before the next big-power summit was about to take place, Khrushchev called the incident an example of U.S. duplicity and "treacherousness." He didn't receive the sought-after apology from Ike and so left the Paris meeting. But he did manage to secure a promise that the flights would be discontinued, and they were. Later on, the Soviets pressed forward their humiliating campaign in the highly publicized espionage trial of Powers. (In February 1962, the CIA pilot was exchanged for high-ranking Soviet spy Rudolf Abel.)

With the U-2 affair a thing of the past, the Eisenhower administration had faced its last great crisis. Like many earlier crises handled by Ike and Dulles, it had ended, if not entirely happily, at least without catastrophe.

As time has gone on, Eisenhower's reputation as a leader in the cold war has grown considerably. For it was on Ike's watch that the ground rules of the superpower relationship really took hold. With his reassuring mixture of practicality, resolve, and steadfastness, he had taken the steps to keep the war in Korea limited. He showed that the United States could solve cold war crises with skill and without resorting to force, even when the Soviets were directly involved.

As he left office, Ike spoke with great wisdom about the dangers of allowing the "military-industrial complex" too much sway in American life. Together with his Soviet counterpart, he opened, at least slightly, the channels of communication between Washington and Moscow, and they would prove vital in averting nuclear war in the years to come. It was a fine and noble thing, Ike seemed to say, to press for the expansion of democratic institutions around the world. But it was perhaps equally important to remember that when it came to national rivalries, overzealousness could lead to disaster.

It was a considerable legacy. What would a young Democratic senator from Massachusetts, John F. Kennedy, do with it? In November 1960, Kennedy was elected president by a narrow margin over Vice President Richard M. Nixon. The first Roman Catholic to be elected to the presidency faced many of the same cold war problems Dwight David Eisenhower and Harry S Truman had confronted. Kennedy was young, the youngest man elected to hold the office. He was also tough and very bright. He had big plans for his nation and its role in the complicated world of the 1960s.

CHAPTER SEVEN

JOHN F. KENNEDY:
THE NEW FRONTIER
AND CUBA

The new administration arrived in Washington in January 1961 with unprecedented fanfare. The dashing young president, only forty-three years old, lost no time in distancing himself from the cautious, conservative style of his predecessor. "The torch has been passed to a new generation of Americans," said Kennedy in his inaugural address. People everywhere sensed that remarkable things were in the offing. A man of great charm, wit, and considerable intellect, Kennedy had grown up in a political family and had been groomed for high achievement. People liked this man. With his glamorous wife, Jackie, only thirty-one years old, by his side, he seemed a fitting symbol for a new and more optimistic era for the United States.

For all its high and glamorous style, the Kennedy team was infused with a toughness of spirit and an abiding faith that all the world admired American democracy and its underlying ideas and institutions and that the United States had an obligation to expand the boundaries of the democratic world. It was an attitude aptly summarized in another memorable line from JFK's inaugural speech: "[We] shall pay any price, bear any burden, meet any hardship, support any friend, oppose any foe to assure the survival and success of liberty."

JFK shared his predecessor's basic assumptions about the cold war. The expansive tendencies of the Communist world suffocated freedom and had to be constrained. "The enemy is the Communist system itself," he told a Salt Lake City audience in 1959, "implacable, insatiable, unceasing in its drive for world domination."[1] Like Eisenhower, Kennedy was committed to dealing with the Kremlin from a position of strength. He felt, however, that Ike had been unimaginative in his approach. The country had relied too long on the perilous crutch of nuclear weapons as a deterrent to Communist aggression. It was important, in an age in which the world was every day becoming more interconnected, to develop other kinds of deterrents.

Just a few weeks before inauguration day, Premier Khrushchev had reaffirmed his nation's intention to support "wars of national liberation." The speech went down very badly in Washington. It seemed a veiled declaration of war against the Western powers, voiced by a man whose bearing and demeanor suggested he felt the Soviets were gaining the upper hand. If the United States was going to best the Soviets in world affairs, a more diverse set of tools would be needed.

In the course of the first few months of the Kennedy administration, studies were commissioned to examine alternative defense strategies and new programs aimed at securing friends—and fending off enemies—in what people were now calling the third world: places with little industrial development, such as Africa, Latin America, and Southeast Asia.

The men called by JFK to serve in Washington were bold, astute, and exceptionally accomplished—not unlike the president they served. Most of them were young; few had reached the age of fifty. Many had served as officers in World War II. They had seen firsthand what the United States could accomplish when willpower and the country's vast resources were brought to bear on a problem or crisis.

Arthur M. Schlesinger, Jr., JFK's special assistant, was a Harvard historian of great repute. A native of Massachusetts, as was Kennedy, he had won the coveted Pulitzer Prize for a biography of Andrew Jackson. Schlesinger shared with his boss a belief that the United States should adopt an "unsentimental," highly rational approach to politics, focused on practical solutions, based on sound research.

Robert S. McNamara, known as one of the young "whiz kids" of the business world, was Kennedy's choice for secretary of defense. He was an expert in statistics, a man with a formidable mind, and a highly admired chief executive officer at Ford Motor Company. McNamara was soon hard at work reshaping the Pentagon's bloated bureaucracy and reconfiguring military policy to meet the new challenges of the 1960s.

Perhaps the most brilliant of the men surrounding the president was McGeorge Bundy, who held the position of special assistant for national security affairs, a post he helped to transform into one of the most powerful in Washington. Born into a patrician New England family, Bundy had graduated first in his class from Yale. He had gone on to edit the memoirs of the father of the American foreign-policy establishment, Henry L. Stimson. After that, he taught government at Harvard and then became the youngest dean of the college in the school's long history. Bundy's assistant was the prolific author Walter Rostow, another academic who had a strong interest in both economics and the politics of guerrilla warfare. Kennedy once joked that Walt could write faster than he could think.

The self-effacing Dean Rusk, a tough but soft-spoken Rhodes scholar from Georgia, was the new secretary of state. He enjoyed the enthusiastic support of the high-powered banking and law communities in Washington and New York. Rusk, who frequently served as the president's point man, won the difficult assignment of re-invigorating the State Department, which had become overly cautious and ineffective in the late 1950s.

The Kennedy foreign-policy team christened their new group of policies the "New Frontier." At its core lay the notion that scholar-general Maxwell Taylor had coined: *flexible response.* Rostow explained it:

> It should be noted that we have generally been at a disadvantage in crises since the Communists command a more flexible set of tools for impos-

ing strain on the Free World—and a greater freedom to use them—than we normally command. . . .We must seek, therefore, to expand our arsenal of . . . countermeasures if we are in fact to make crisis-mongering, deeply built into Communist ideology and working habits, an unprofitable occupation.[2]

Some of the new "tools" were designed to head off third world grievances through economic and social aid programs. The Peace Corps sent young, idealistic Americans into developing nations to teach basic skills, such as better methods of farming, and to build schools and plumbing systems. In March 1961, the president proposed the Alliance for Progress, an international organization funded largely by the United States to improve the economic status of Western Hemisphere (mainly Latin American) countries.

Flexible response had a significant military component. The defense budget rose from $43 billion to $56 billion a year during JFK's three years in office. The Polaris and Minuteman ICBM missile programs, vastly more accurate than the old Atlases, were stepped up. In 1961 alone, 300,000 people were added to the U.S. armed forces, part of a general buildup of conventional forces deemed essential by McNamara and Kennedy. The president took a personal interest in the training of the U.S. Army's new Special Forces soldiers, known as the Green Berets. They were experts at counterinsurgency, trained to fight leftist guerrillas at their own game.

JFK had always felt that the Republicans had neglected the peculiar problems that attended fighting the cold war in the third world; it was somehow fitting that his first real test of leadership came in an operation involving a third world nation, and one that was a neighbor to the United States, no less.

From 1933 to 1944, a former Cuban army sergeant, Fulgencio Batista, ran Cuba with an iron hand. He was toppled from power briefly, only to reemerge in 1952 as a full-fledged dictator whose major concern was lining his own pockets and those of his associates. During the 1950s American citizens owned a large percentage of Cuban farmland and almost all the means of production. "American commercial interests made no objection to Batista's corrupt authoritarian regime," wrote one historian, "and he in turn protected those interests."[3] Angered by the injustice and corruption of the Cuban government, Fidel Castro and a small band of followers conducted a successful guerrilla war against Batista from their mountain base in the Sierra Maestra. On January 1, 1959, to the delight of the vast majority of Cubans, Castro ousted Batista from Havana.

The initial reaction of the U.S. government was cautious. The United States had thought Batista a liability since at least the beginning of 1958. Official recognition was granted the Castro government just a week after Batista went into exile. A number of American companies advanced Castro a total of $1.5 million in funds to help stabilize the country. Then, just a month or so after assuming power, Castro began a long series of public executions of policemen and military officers of the

Batista regime. Protests erupted in the U.S. Congress and across the United States. Castro responded angrily, claiming quite correctly that the United States had not been much bothered by the torture and killing conducted under Batista.

The relations between the two countries grew more problematic when Castro appointed a number of Communists to the Cuban security agencies, including the secret police. In June 1959, the Cuban leader began a series of land reforms. Part of the reform package involved taking over, without compensation, lands owned by such American concerns as the United Fruit Company, further aggravating the relations between the two countries. The Cuban government also seized several American-owned oil refineries that had refused to refine Soviet oil, then took over many big businesses. In 1960 a high Soviet official, Anastas Mikoyan, visited Castro. Then came a trade agreement between the two countries and a trip by Castro to Czechoslovakia to purchase arms. In October 1960 the United States banned all American exports to Cuba except for food and medicine; all American purchases of Cuban sugar and tobacco were stopped.

Soon, shipments of rifles, rockets, and mortars were flowing into the island nation from Eastern Europe and the Soviet Union. In late 1960, with the approval of the Eisenhower administration, the CIA had begun to train a brigade of Cuban exiles in Florida for an invasion of the island. Their objective: to spark a general uprising against Castro's regime.

After being briefed by CIA head of covert operations

Richard Bissell, President Kennedy gave the green light for the invasion. On the morning of April 15, 1961, six World War II–vintage B-26 bombers, flown from bases in Nicaragua by Cuban pilots, attacked the Cuban Air Force on the ground, hoping to diminish Castro's ability to halt the amphibious assault that was to follow. Members of Brigade 2506 disembarked from their landing craft at 1:15 A.M. on April 17. Unexpected coral reefs in Cuba's Bay of Pigs slowed the landing, and much of the heavy equipment, including tanks, never made it ashore. The landing force, which consisted of about fourteen hundred men, was rapidly pinned down by heavy artillery fire and by strafing from Cuban T-33 jet trainers.

Intelligence reports indicated that all that could save the force from disaster would be the intervention of U.S. jets and ground forces. Kennedy, conferring with his key foreign-policy advisers, decided against such an action. It might give the Soviets an excuse for further operations in Berlin, or elsewhere.

By April 20, the brigade, having expended most of its ammunition and lacking air cover, had been routed. One hundred fourteen invaders died in the fighting; the remainder were taken prisoner. Castro's losses have been estimated to be about sixteen hundred killed in action.

Once it was clear that the attack had been sponsored by the CIA, anti-American demonstrations erupted throughout Latin America. Castro released 1,189 Bay of Pigs prisoners in December 1962 in exchange for $62 million in food and medicine, which had been raised by private sources in the United States.

President Kennedy took full responsibility for the

debacle, although recent scholarship suggests that the CIA plan was based on overly optimistic assessments of what the exiles could accomplish. The failure of the raid prompted the retirement of a number of CIA officials, including Director Allen Dulles and Richard Bissell, who had done much of the planning. The Bay of Pigs venture marked the end of what historians have called the "golden age of covert action" for the CIA.

The Bay of Pigs was the second foreign-policy humiliation for the United States within a year. The bad judgment of Kennedy and his experts underscored the grave difficulties of carrying out the anti-Communist crusade. Not everybody—certainly not most Cubans in 1961—was looking to be "rescued" by the Central Intelligence Agency or its hired guns. Indeed, the uproar that swept through Latin America after the Bay of Pigs debacle suggested that the United States and its new president had much to learn about politics and power in the third world. The fiasco lent credence to the views of many Latin Americans, who felt, as the historian Norman Graebner put it, that "American policy was designed to create maximum change behind the Iron Curtain, and to prevent it elsewhere."[4]

Soon after the news of the Bay of Pigs disaster reached the world, a Soviet agent, Georgi Bolshakov, arranged for a meeting with U.S. Attorney General Robert ("Bobby") Kennedy, the brother of the president. Bolshakov told Bobby Kennedy that much could be gained by a meeting between JFK and Khrushchev. Did the president's proposal for a summit, issued the previous February, still stand? It did. It was agreed that the two men would meet the following June in Vienna, the capital of neutral Austria.

Ominous developments in the Southeast Asian nation of Laos occupied the attention of Americans and Soviets alike. The Communists in Laos, the Pathet Lao, were on the offensive against a U.S.-sponsored government. By April 1961 more than three hundred U.S. military advisers were there, but the Communist forces were stronger and better organized than those of the royalist, pro-American government. As June approached, the Pathet Lao controlled the eastern half of the country. Kennedy ruled out the deployment of U.S. troops and used diplomatic and economic incentives to bring the disparate forces together into a coalition government. From the point of view of cold war politics, Laos was a stalemate.

With the situation in Laos resolved for the time being, the presidential entourage headed for Vienna. There was to be a stop in Paris on the way; JFK wanted to confer with the imperious French president, Charles de Gaulle. De Gaulle made it clear that France would not accept American leadership in the matter of the defense of Europe. He intended to develop his own, independent nuclear arsenal. When the conversation turned to Indochina, the French leader offered sound advice, saying that Southeast Asia was no place for a Western army to fight: Vietnam was a bottomless military and political quagmire, and it would be a losing battle.

In Vienna, JFK met Khrushchev with the intention of diminishing tensions between the superpowers. It was an unfulfilled goal. About all that could be agreed on was that the cold war should be kept out of Laos. Much time was expended in verbal duels in which each leader tried to establish the superiority of his respective political and social system. This went nowhere. As JFK later remarked, he and Khrushchev didn't speak the same language.

It was certainly the case that they did not speak the same language concerning the city of Berlin. Khrushchev demanded a new four-power conference to discuss the temporary arrangements agreed to at the end of World War II. Again he threatened to sign a separate peace with East Germany and to turn over control of the West Berlin access routes to East Germany, which was not formally bound to keep them open. The Soviet leader, under pressure from Kremlin hard-liners, sought to push the young American president into a corner. Either the West would negotiate on Berlin, he seemed to say, or else . . .

Khrushchev pressed hard for a simple reason. Berlin was like a bleeding sore to the Soviet Union. The Soviet leader once described the Western sector of the city as "a bone in my throat." In the first six months of 1961, 150,000 East Germans left their families and friends behind to seek opportunity in the West. They simply walked into West Berlin. And on top of this, Western access to the city also provided the CIA with a wealth of intelligence about Soviet and East German activities.

JFK was genuinely disturbed by Khrushchev's tough stance. But so soon after the Bay of Pigs, was it possible to begin negotiations without appearing weak and ineffectual? It didn't seem so. Kennedy's response was measured but firm: The United States had to honor its obligation to preserve freedom in Berlin. If it failed to do so, JFK told Khrushchev, "U.S. commitments would be regarded as a mere scrap of paper. Western Europe is vital to our national security. . . . If we were to leave West Berlin, Europe would be abandoned as well."[5]

The Soviet leader was unimpressed with this reasoning. He gave the West six months to negotiate a solution; otherwise, he would sign the treaty with East Germany (the German Democratic Republic, or GDR). As the Vienna talks went on, the Soviet leader resorted to bullying tactics. He banged his hand down on the table and shouted at Kennedy, "I want peace. But if you want war, that is your problem."[6]

Upon Kennedy's return to the United States, the administration turned its attention to other difficult questions. Was the Soviet leader bluffing? Was he attempting to intimidate the United States? Should Kennedy send a division of troops toward the East German border to show his resolve? Was it possible to negotiate through normal diplomatic channels? As the president and his advisers wrestled with these issues, Secretary of Defense McNamara set to work preparing a nuclear first-strike plan. The clock kept ticking. . . .

After considerable reflection, JFK decided on a plan that would send a strong signal to Moscow. He requested more than $3 billion for a buildup of conventional military forces and announced his readiness to implement an airlift to support Berlin's Western sector. United States forces were put on alert around the world. While he stopped short of declaring a state of emergency, the president left few doubts that any Communist move against the Western sector of the city of Berlin would trigger a ferocious response. On July 25, he informed the American people that an attack on Berlin would be "regarded as an attack upon us all."[7]

It worked. All talk of passing control of Berlin to East Germany ceased. But on August 13, 1961, Russian and East German troops responded: they erected a barbed-wire barrier around the circumference of their sector, entirely sealing it off from the West. Over the next few days, when they saw that the Western powers were doing nothing to stop them, they began to build a concrete wall. In October, Khrushchev called off his December deadline for a Soviet–East German peace treaty that might have led to Western ejection from Berlin. The immediate crisis thus ended.

The Berlin Wall solved one embarrassing problem for the Soviets—it was no longer possible for East Germans, by going through East Berlin, to take their labor and their skills to West Berlin and the capitalist world. But the wall did nothing to address the fundamental imbalance in nuclear forces between the U.S. and USSR that so haunted Moscow and worried the rest of the world.

The Soviet premier was under increasing pressure from hard-liners in Moscow and from the Chinese, who felt that he had not been tough enough with the capitalists. In mid-1961, the United States had at its disposal about a thousand planes capable of dropping nuclear bombs, forty ICBMs (intercontinental ballistic missiles), and a hundred intermediate-range nuclear missiles deployed in Europe. For its part, the Soviet Union had two hundred bombers, all of inferior quality to those of the United States, and perhaps ten ICBMs, which were less accurate than those at Washington's disposal. The numerical problem would take years for the USSR to adjust. The strategic balance, however, could be changed quickly. The method was simple: Put nuclear missiles off the coast of the United States—in Cuba. That is exactly what Khrushchev did.

On October 14, 1962, a U.S. spy plane took photographs of western Cuba that revealed the presence of offensive missile launchers of Soviet origin. The photos shocked JFK: the Soviets had promised not to place such weapons outside the borders of the Soviet Union after U.S. diplomats had made it clear that any such deployment would be seen as a direct threat to American security. Having made his position clear on Soviet offensive missiles generally, Kennedy couldn't dismiss their presence in the Western Hemisphere as having only a marginal impact on the balance of strategic forces. (In fact, the experts now agree that even with missiles in Cuba the United States still enjoyed an immense strategic advantage.)

The nuclear balance, though, was not the only thing at stake. In addition, there was the delicate matter of prestige. How would the United States look if it was known that it let the Soviet missile deployment go unchecked? Kennedy quickly assembled a group of advisers to help him fashion a response to the Soviet move. For the next two weeks these men—McGeorge Bundy, Dean Rusk, Robert McNamara, Bobby Kennedy, and others—worked under enormous strain to force the

Russians to back off. This was the cold war at it most perilous point. Every one of the advisers was aware, as the President put it, that "if we make a mistake there may be 200 million dead."[8]

During the first tense day of meetings, "Ex Comm" (short for Executive Committee, as the working group was called) proposed two possible courses of action. Maxwell Taylor and Dean Rusk pressed for a surprise attack, an air strike designed to take out the missile sites before they could be made operational. Such a course would have removed the immediate possibility of Moscow stalling until it actually had weapons emplaced and then using them as bargaining chips. But an attack entailed great risks, including reprisal by Russian troops against a NATO country. It was also true that success couldn't be guaranteed. Air strikes did not have pin-point accuracy.

The alternative approach called for no military response whatsoever. Adlai Stevenson, the United States' ambassador to the United Nations, took the lead in calling for negotiations through diplomatic channels. Perhaps an exchange could be worked out: U.S. missiles could be removed from Turkey, near the Soviet border, in exchange for the removal of Soviet missiles from Cuba. It was a less dramatic plan than the Rusk-Taylor proposal, but it, too, entailed problems. Diplomatic negotiations would be slow and possibly painful. It promised no relief from the immediate danger, which troubled all Americans: Soviet-built nuclear missiles might soon be able to reach U.S. cities within five minutes of launch time. If negotiations were pursued, it was inevitable that the peoples of the world would soon learn of the crisis, further complicating a situation that might spin out of control at any minute. JFK was thus understandably reluctant to go public at this point.

For several days, the debate ground on in secrecy. The public first caught wind of the crisis on October 22, when a weary John Kennedy went on national television to alert the nation and the world to the situation. The president pulled no punches. He began by saying that "unmistakable evidence" had established the presence of offensive weapons in Cuba. Their purpose was to give the Soviet Union a nuclear strike capacity against the Western hemisphere. It was "an explicit threat to the peace and security of the Americas," and it had been put into place after recent assurances from Khrushchev that no such missiles would be deployed.

Kennedy announced that he had ordered a naval quarantine of the island: No ship would be allowed access to Cuba's ports. No offensive military equipment would be allowed to make its way to shore from any Soviet vessel (a number of which were cruising toward Cuba at that time). Kennedy exhorted his Soviet counterpart to move the world back from the brink of destruction. The ball was now in Khrushchev's court.

On the morning of October 23, millions of people awoke delighted—delighted to be alive. The quarantine went into effect on October 24. As Ex Comm listened to events over the U.S. Navy radio network, a Soviet submarine approached, coming menacingly close to the quarantine line. But it made no move to cross, and around 10:30 A.M. came the first of several hopeful messages: Russian ships heading toward Cuba had halted. The news prompted Dean Rusk, the self-effacing secretary of state, to utter the now-famous words "We're eyeball to eyeball, and I think the other fellow just blinked."[9]

The Soviets would respect the blockade. One phase of the Cuban Missile Crisis was over. Now the focus shifted: Would the Russians continue work on the missile launchers? It appeared that they would. The hardliners in Ex Comm pressed for rapid military action; the Soviets clearly intended to obtain the added leverage that missile-launching capability would deliver.

Throughout the agonizing two weeks of crisis, messages were transmitted through several sources. Khrushchev wrote a rambling letter to JFK, passionately arguing for peace and saying that the Soviets could not allow the blockade to continue without a military response. Khrushchev called on the United States to lift the blockade. He had a proposal. If the United States would promise never to invade Cuba, he would withdraw the missiles and promise never to redeploy them.

But on the morning of Saturday, October 27, before Kennedy had prepared a reply, came another communication, this one via radio. More formally worded, it restated the claim that the Soviet Union had every right to deploy nuclear weapons in Cuba. The ante was upped—somewhat. The new proposal offered withdrawal of the Cuban missiles in exchange for withdrawal of U.S. Jupiter missiles in Turkey.

The missiles in Turkey were almost obsolete; Kennedy had already indicated that he planned to remove them in the near future (and did so). Yet there would be grave difficulties in accepting such a clear trade-off. The proposal struck some of the advisers as a clever ploy to shake the NATO nations' faith in the United States. The impression that the Americans were bargaining over missiles in this way would have gone over very badly in Europe. Many might believe the United States had been outmaneuvered.

That afternoon, a U-2 pilot flying over Cuba was shot down and killed by an antiaircraft missile. It was soon determined that the shooting was undertaken independently by some jittery Soviet officers on the ground; it hadn't been ordered by Moscow. But for a short while, the incident convinced Kennedy that he would soon have to order an air strike.

Since the president couldn't appear to be bargaining over missiles, he indicated, through secret channels, that he would pledge not to invade Cuba in exchange for the removal of the missiles. But no "deal" could be made concerning the missiles in Turkey. That would have to be negotiated after the Soviets agreed to remove the weapons and pledge never to bring them back. JFK issued a public letter stating his terms.

Finally, on the morning of October 28, a Sunday, Ex Comm received the anxiously awaited response. Khrushchev drafted the reply himself:

I have received your message of October 27. I express my satisfaction and thank you for the sense of proportion you have displayed and for recognition of the responsibility you now bear for the preservation of the peace of the world. I very well understand your anxiety and that of the American people about the fact that the weapons you describe as offensive are formidable weapons indeed. . . .

In order to eliminate as rapidly as possible the conflict which endangers the cause of peace . . . the Soviet Government, in addition to previously issued instructions to cease further work on weapons construction sites, has issued a new order to dismantle the weapons which you describe as offensive, and to crate and return them to the Soviet Union. . . .[10]

The Cuban Missile Crisis enforced the idea that the world could go up in smoke and how vital it was for the two superpowers to restrain and regulate their rivalry. Everyone privy to the critical decisions of the crisis knew that at several junctures the world was within hours, if not minutes, of outright war. That, of course, was what had made the whole situation so profoundly serious, so exhausting. Both sides had issued what amounted to direct military threats, and they had meant them.

John Kennedy had gained the admiration and respect of people throughout the world, but he, like Khrushchev, was sobered by the experience of taking the world to the brink. Before Cuba, high-ranking officials of the United States often bragged about American military superiority. After the missile crisis, there was considerably less boasting. The Soviets, too, toned down their rhetoric, and there was an unmistakable willingness to de-escalate tensions all around. A telephone hot line was installed between the two heads of state by the following summer. In August 1963, the United States, the USSR, and Britain signed the Limited Nuclear Test Ban Treaty, which the U.S. Senate ratified in September.

There were other reverberations. The missile crisis established the importance—and legitimacy, at least so far as the superpowers' governments were concerned—of "spheres of influence." After Cuba, the Soviets never again tried to place nuclear weapons in the Western Hemisphere. It was equally clear that the United States would not attempt to break the Soviet hold on Eastern Europe by military intervention.

Although the Cuban Missile Crisis did much for JFK's reputation, it amounted to a humiliation of the first rank for Khrushchev. Historians mark the beginning of his decline in power with his failure to gain a victory in Cuba. Before the Soviet leader was to leave the world stage in 1964, however, Kennedy would meet a tragic end, the victim of an assassin's bullet in Dallas, Texas, on November 22, 1963.

In the last year of his life and his presidency, John Kennedy and his policy makers had become increasingly preoccupied with a problem that did not lend itself to simple solutions: the war in Vietnam. The Communists under the leadership of Ho Chi Minh were pressing forward with their insurgency against an unpopular, struggling regime in the South. The Vietminh of the First Indochina War were now called the Vietcong. Their objective, however, was the same as it had always been: They sought to unite all Vietnam under the rule of Hanoi.

The government of South Vietnam had been shaped and supported by the United States. For their part, the South Vietnamese were calling for a higher level of American assistance to combat the increasingly aggressive (and successful) Communists. More and more, it was clear that the United States was determined to hold the line against North Vietnamese pressure, no matter what it cost, no matter how vast the difficulties in fashioning a strong, democratic government in the South. Few foresaw what loomed on the horizon. The U.S. commitment to South Vietnam was on the verge of mushrooming into an American war of major proportions with profound consequences for the cold war.

CHAPTER EIGHT

COLD WAR TRAGEDY: THE WAR IN VIETNAM

I t was unfortunate that America's great anti-Communist crusade of the 1960s unfolded on the peninsula of Indochina, in the former French colony of Vietnam. Vietnam was a very poor country with a rich history, but one bereft of democratic tradition. In the late 1950s and early 1960s, the Republic of Vietnam (South Vietnam) was under the iron rule of President Ngo Dinh Diem. Diem, an imperious Catholic with many influential supporters in the United States, including Francis Cardinal Spellman and John F. Kennedy (from 1953 to 1960 a senator from Massachusetts), was hardly a leader of inspiring stature. Dressed in an impeccable white suit, he would receive diplomats and advisers in the presidential palace in Saigon, talking endlessly, never bothering to listen, especially when the Americans came with bad news or complaints.

Indeed, Diem's foremost concern rested not with the welfare of his people, for he seemed monumentally indifferent to their fate. His passion lay in keeping tabs on political rivals. It was not an easy job. Saigon, the capital of South Vietnam, always seemed awash in a sea of intrigue. The growing Communist insurgency within South Vietnam's borders, the rampant government corruption, the looting of the tax coffers, much of which was carried out by Diem's own family—none of it seemed worthy of Diem's attention.

He did, however, have one characteristic that attracted high officials of the U.S. government: He was fervently anti-Communist. Thus it was that both Eisenhower and Kennedy tended to minimize his many shortcomings. Both presidents sought to bolster the regime by making up for Diem's lethargy and incompetence with money and an advisory effort (on civil as well as military matters) of increasing magnitude.

American aid had been flowing into the Republic of Vietnam since its inception in 1954. By 1960 the United States had sunk more than $1 billion into South Vietnam, and in the next years the investment grew steadily. John Kennedy responded to stepped-up Vietcong activity within the borders of South Vietnam by increasing the number of military advisers from about nine hundred men at the beginning of 1961 to some sixteen thousand at the time of his assassination in 1963. Many of these advisers were members of the U.S. Army's Green Berets: highly trained soldiers who had studied the ways of guerrilla warfare.

All of this U.S. aid helped avert the collapse of

Diem's government, albeit temporarily. It hardly solved the deeply entrenched problems of South Vietnam: It was a poor nation under attack from a powerful insurgency. Over time Diem came to see, quite correctly, that as the American commitment deepened, Washington needed him just as much as he needed Washington. American prestige depended on things going well in South Vietnam, and Diem called the shots there. Thus he was able to preserve a regime that was listless and out of touch with its people far longer than he might otherwise have done. Journalists sometimes jokingly said that Diem was an American "puppet who pulled his own strings."

Indeed, Diem and his handpicked top officials (most were relatives) grew complacent, believing that American money and weapons would succeed in crushing the will of the Vietcong. Diem and company could meanwhile continue to plunder the country, extracting bribes, stealing matériel sent by the United States, preserving their positions of privilege. And plunder and abuse it they did.

The officers of the Army of the Republic of Vietnam (the ARVN) were singularly ill equipped to lead a peasant army raised from the countryside. Almost to a man they were from the privileged class, from families in the large cities of Saigon and Hue with connections to the old French aristocracy. They cared nothing for the poor. Graft, fraud, and corruption were rampant in the army and, in fact, in all South Vietnamese political agencies. American goods were often commandeered by ARVN officers and sold for a 300 to 400 percent profit to the Vietcong. Fighting was not a high priority in the ARVN.

This was proved conclusively at the Battle of Ap Bac in January 1963, when highly mobile, heavily armed ARVN soldiers were outclassed by lightly armed Vietcong guerrillas. U.S. Army adviser John Paul Vann resigned in disgust after the battle.* The South Vietnamese officers had deliberately turned away from a fight with the Vietcong, fearing their own deaths. And what was worse, the United States was looking the other way, failing to insist that Diem and his army commit themselves to the fight.

Eventually, Diem's intransigence and ineptitude caught up with him. In November of 1963, a few weeks before JFK was killed, the South Vietnamese president was murdered in a coup organized by ARVN officers and approved, or at least not objected to, by the U.S. embassy in Saigon. From that time, South Vietnam was ruled by a series of unimaginative, uninspiring military regimes propped up by the United States. One journalist wrote in 1970 that "after all these years of war, the Saigon government remains a network of cliques, held together by American subsidies, a group of people without a coherent political orientation, bent on their own survival."[1]

In the United States, direction of the increasingly problematic American involvement fell to one of the masters of domestic politics, President Lyndon Baines Johnson, who was from Texas. It was not a war that LBJ (as Johnson was known) had a burning desire to fight. He wanted above all else to fight poverty and injustice at

*A *Bright Shining Lie,* a fascinating book about Vann and Vietnam, was written by Neil Sheehan.

home, not Communist expansionism abroad. But like John Kennedy, Johnson believed that America's position as leader of the free world required it to hold the line against Communist aggression. Just a few days after taking the presidential oath of office, the Texan told Henry Cabot Lodge, the U.S. ambassador in Saigon, that he wasn't about to "lose Vietnam." He went on to instruct the patrician diplomat to "tell those generals in Saigon that Lyndon Johnson intends to stand by our word" that the United States wouldn't let the Communists take over the country.[2]

Johnson's thinking about the struggle against communism had been shaped (much like Eisenhower's and Kennedy's) by his understanding of the infamous Munich agreement before World War II. It was at Munich that Britain agreed to cede a part of Czechoslovakia to Nazi Germany in the hope of satisfying Germany's desire for European territory. Johnson believed that appeasement in Munich had fed, not quenched, Hitler's thirst for land. Soon after assuming office, President Johnson spoke plainly, telling the American people that "the battle against communism must be joined in Southeast Asia with strength and determination . . . or the United States, inevitably, must surrender the Pacific and take up our defenses on our own shores."[3]

From the moment of his assumption of the presidency, Vietnam was the critical foreign-policy issue of the Johnson years (1963–69). In late December 1963, Secretary of State McNamara warned the new president

HO CHI MINH TRAIL

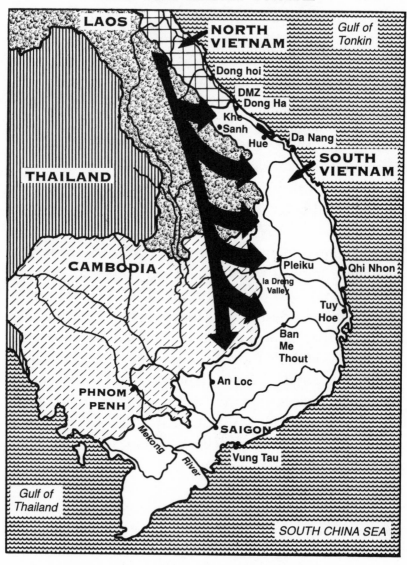

that unless major changes were made, and made quickly, South Vietnam would soon fall. The American team stationed there, consisting of both military and civilian advisers, lacked strong leadership and clear direction. After much reflection and discussion, Johnson acted. He appointed a square-jawed paratrooper, General William Westmoreland, to head an expanded U.S. military command in South Vietnam. And he increased the number of advisers (technically, Americans were not allowed to fight in Vietnam until 1965) to twenty-three thousand. The president also approved commando raids into North Vietnamese territory by South Vietnamese troops with U.S. military advisers.

As supplies and troops from North Vietnam trickled down the Ho Chi Minh Trail (a complicated network of trails and roads running along the eastern edge of Vietnam's neighbors Laos and Cambodia) a fateful episode occurred—or reportedly occurred—off the coast of North Vietnam in the Gulf of Tonkin. Johnson administration officials claimed that the U.S. destroyer *Maddox* was attacked by North Vietnamese patrol boats. Two days later, on August 4, 1964, another attack on the *Maddox* and on a companion ship, the *Turner Joy*, was reported by the U.S. Navy. These two incidents set the stage for an expanded war, as LBJ called upon Congress to approve the Gulf of Tonkin Resolution of August 7, 1964. The resolution gave the president extraordinary powers hitherto unheard of in U.S. history. The chief executive was authorized to "take all necessary measures to repel any armed attack against the forces of the United States and to prevent further aggression." It was, in essence, a blank check, but it was not a declaration of war as sanctioned by the U.S. Constitution.

Then came two decisions that drew the nation into Vietnam in earnest. In February 1965, after eight U.S. servicemen lost their lives in a Vietcong (VC) attack on a South Vietnamese air base in Pleiku, the president ordered retaliatory air strikes against targets within North Vietnam. The air raids, officially part of Operation Rolling Thunder, continued through November 1968.

In March 1965 the first regular U.S. ground troops waded ashore in Vietnam. No one at the time made much of the deployment of these fifteen hundred U.S. Marines; they were sent to guard an air base at Da Nang from which elements of the American and South Vietnamese air forces operated. But soon their mission was changed, and the marines began to run patrols around the base, in search of the enemy. By the end of 1965, more than 180,000 American troops were in Southeast Asia; combat was on the upswing, and the United States was once again in a hot war against communism.

Critics of the war have often depicted the high-level decision makers in Washington as reckless warmongers determined to push the United States into the fight against Ho Chi Minh as quickly as possible. There were some "hawks" raring to go to war, but they were in the minority in the Johnson administration, which in fact made each decision to escalate U.S. involvement only after painstaking debate. Like his predecessors all the way back to Harry Truman, LBJ sought, at every juncture, to do what was necessary to avoid defeat, not to secure victory.

Indeed, the major goal of the Americans in 1964 and 1965 was not so much to crush the Communists as to pressure them into a settlement that would preserve the independence of South Vietnam. John Kennedy had been worried that a full-scale commitment in Vietnam might bring the Chinese into the conflict. It had happened in Korea. LBJ believed the same thing. He was also nervous about what action the Soviets might take. "We don't want a wider war," he once explained. "They [the North Vietnamese] have two big brothers [China and the USSR] that have more weight and people than I have."[4]

This strange and unique approach to war was in many ways the product of McNamara's ideas and outlook. The secretary of defense, with his team of Pentagon consultants, believed that war could be successfully managed using the sophisticated tools of computers, systems analysis, and statistics. MacNamara, observed historian Bernard Weisberger,

> loved to deal with this technician's war in the cool precision of statistics, so many weapons and troops involved, so many hamlets [villages] secured, so many Viet Cong eliminated. The "body count" became a yardstick of success. One could develop figures on the various "kill ratios" of dead to wounded, firepower to total casualties, dollars to dead enemies.[5]

It was one of the many ironies of the war that this approach, intended to give the United States maximum flexibility and leverage, backfired. For in focusing on the piecemeal commitments, the body counts, and the wealth of statistics concerning kill ratios and the like, LBJ and his advisers lost sight of the fact that the preservation of South Vietnam was not a vital interest of the United States. Nor did they see that while American forces were inflicting heavy casualties on the enemy, Hanoi's will remained unaffected by the American war effort. The huge number of casualties suffered by both the Vietcong (the "irregular" Communist soldiers, mostly natives of the southern half of Vietnam) and the North Vietnamese Army had little effect on the situation on the ground, for the dead and the wounded were quickly replaced with fresh, highly motivated troops.

Shortly before his death, John Kennedy had said that in the end it was up to the South Vietnamese to win the war. By 1966, however, all that kept South Vietnam together was the vast and still growing U.S. financial and military investment in the country. American goods flooded the black market, and more and more, the U.S. Army and Marines took the initiative in fighting the Vietcong. American units of battalion size (about nine hundred men) were combing the deltas, highlands, and jungles, engaging Communist troops in "search and destroy" missions. General Westmoreland hoped to crush the will of the Communists by finding enemy units and rapidly converging on them with a stunning array of modern weapons: artillery, helicopter gunships, and jets, which could drop cluster bombs (explosives that sent shards of hot metal flying over a wide area) and napalm alike. Infantry could then be brought in to finish off the job.

However, for the soldiers, and for the American public who for the first time could watch recent, almost daily combat on television, it seemed a war without clear lines or objectives, a war against what one CBS reporter described as "the most faceless foe in our history."[6] Faceless, but very determined and difficult to root out. The Vietcong preferred to launch surprise attacks on U.S. units and then disappear into the jungle rather than to press the fight and run the (great) risk that U.S. artillery would zero in on their position and decimate their ranks.

The soldier of the night ambush might be the simple rice farmer of the day. This fading away of the enemy naturally led to a great deal of trouble between the villagers, the vast majority of whom had no interest in politics, and U.S. soldiers, who had been taught they were in Vietnam to save these same villagers from the horrors of communism. The Vietnamese peasants, even those who hated the Vietcong, resented the foreign presence. Many actually mistook the Americans for the returning French, who for more than a hundred years had exploited and abused the people of Vietnam.

Soldiers and marines sent out to patrol the countryside during operations sometimes had to carry as much as sixty pounds of gear and ammunition, often in oppressive heat, mud, and rain. Vietnam was the first American war to be fought without front lines, that is, without a clear distinction between one's own territory and the enemy's. Therefore, combat could (and did) break out in the most surprising of places, including Saigon, the beautiful, French-built city that was the capital of South Vietnam and the seat of U.S. power. Ambushes were common, as were booby traps and mines that lay in wait for the tired "grunts," as the foot soldiers were called. Booby traps of one sort or another were responsible for more than 10 percent of the fifty-eight thousand deaths suffered by U.S. troops from 1959 to 1973.

Those soldiers who bore the brunt of the fight in Vietnam suffered from special burdens in many ways unique in the annals of American military history. "They did not know the feeling of taking a place and keeping it," wrote Tim O'Brien, an army infantry veteran, in one of his novels.

No front, no rear, no trenches laid out in neat parallels, no Patton rushing for the Rhine, no beachheads to storm and win and hold for the duration. They did not have targets, they did not have a cause. . . . On a given day they did not know where they were in Quang Ngai or how being there might influence larger outcomes.[7]

In the later years of American involvement, a deep sense of futility developed among those who did the ground fighting. One measure of this truth: The number and intensity of the firefights in Vietnam dropped off in the last couple of years of the war, but the psychiatric casualty rates shot upward during this same period, as did the use of illicit drugs and alcohol and the number of incidents in which officers were shot by their own men.

The most common image of the war in films is that of well-armed Americans tangling with elusive, "pajama-clad" guerrillas. In fact, the fighting took many other forms. By the end, many of the half million U.S. troops in Vietnam fought against highly trained regular army troops that had come to the South via the Ho Chi Minh Trail as replacements for the Vietcong irregulars. The North Vietnamese Army (NVA) carried out hundreds of conventional frontal assaults on U.S. positions, many of which blossomed into vicious firefights. A U.S. Marine rifleman, John Muir, described such an assault on the small airfield he was defending with about a hundred other marines near the Demilitarized Zone (DMZ) that ran between North and South Vietnam:

They [the NVA] put artillery up above us and were shooting down right on top of us. Rockets, machine gun fire, rifle fire, everything you want. It was all pointblank.

Helicopters kept resupplying us. They would take a quick low pass at the top of the hill and zoom by there, throwing out water and ammunition, grabbing as many wounded as they could. . . . We really didn't think about the future. I had no expectation of making it out of there. . . . I had written us off. People were too tired to cry. . . . Sometimes [the NVA would] come on a dead run hollering and screaming. Usually they came in well-organized, well-controlled assaults. We knew we were up against professionals; we knew we were up against some good ones.[8]

Such fighting took a heavy toll on the Communist

forces. General Vo Nguyen Giap, chief strategist of the NVA, claimed after the war that between 1964 and 1969 his forces had suffered half a million men killed—nearly ten times the number of American deaths during the entire war. Some military officers pointed to the high Communist body counts as progress. Yet large sectors of the public in the United States took no great pride in the superior killing ability of their troops.

By 1967, the number of dissenting voices, both in official Washington and in the nation generally, was growing. Was Vietnam worth the sacrifice? Would the dominoes fall if the United States pulled out? Were American tactics, with their reliance on massive firepower, actually destroying the country in order to save it? Even if the Americans were able to break the will of the North Vietnamese, would the South Vietnamese be able to put their house in order and build a democratic society?

As 1967 drew to a close, there were many such questions but few convincing answers. A popular sentiment in 1966 and 1967, observed Vietnam historian Ronald Spector, was that "we ought to win or get out. The problem was that the means to either win or get out were as confused and controversial as the war itself."[9] Discontent spread far beyond the university campuses and the liberal community, where it had originated. By the beginning of 1968, about one-quarter of the U.S. House of Representatives had become disenchanted with the war effort. Americans, in addition to struggling with growing student unrest in the colleges, grew more and more weary of a costly conflict in a faraway place without clear objectives.

Despite all these ominous developments—the surprising endurance of the Communists, the lackluster performance of the South Vietnamese, the growing troubles at home that were in part the result of the war itself—Washington offered the press and the nation an upbeat version of the conflict: American units were defeating the enemy on the battlefield on a daily basis; South Vietnam was, the statistics said, making progress on crop production, road and school building, and other public works projects. In November 1967, Westmoreland himself returned home to reassure the people that all was well. The end, he said, was beginning "to come into view."[10]

The tendency to downplay the bad news led to a rift between the press and the government that fueled the "credibility gap," the difference between the official version of events emanating from Washington and what was really happening in Vietnam as observed by reporters on the scene.

The event that blew the credibility gap wide open was the Tet Offensive of January 1968. Launched on the Vietnamese lunar new year, the offensive consisted of scores of simultaneous attacks on South Vietnamese cities, provincial capitals, and military installations. Even the great symbol of American power in Southeast Asia, the embassy in Saigon, was assaulted; a commando team breached the U.S. embassy compound and had to be flushed out by CIA men and military policemen.

There was no doubt about it—Tet caught the United States off guard. For a few hours, American and South Vietnamese troops were on the defensive all over

Vietnam. But within a couple of days, U.S. and ARVN troops had repulsed the attacks just about everywhere, with the exception of the old capital, the city of Hue, where intense fighting persisted until late February. Many of the highly trained Vietcong units that had spearheaded the attacks were decimated in the U.S.–ARVN counterattacks.

Tet, in the end, was a tactical disaster for the Communists. Their recklessness had led to casualties that no Western commander could have allowed. Many of the Vietcong units were virtually wiped out. Vietnam, however, was not like most wars. Strangely enough, Hanoi's tactical defeat amounted to a strategic victory. Why? Because the Communists' ability to launch the attacks convinced millions of people in the United States that the war could not be won by South Vietnam even with a very high level of support and sacrifice by the United States.

By mid-March 1968, approval for President Johnson's handling of the war had plummeted to an all-time low: only twenty-six percent of those polled approved of their president's management of the war. Stanley Karnow observed in his history of the war, "The country's trust in [LBJ's] authority had evaporated. His credibility—the key to a president's capacity to govern—was gone."[11] About one month after the outbreak of Tet, the *Wall Street Journal* ominously warned that "the American people should be getting ready to accept, if they haven't already, the prospect that the whole Vietnam effort may be doomed."[12]

The Tet Offensive and the grim reaction from the

media and the public prompted a searching reexamination of the war by many of the most distinguished members of the U.S. foreign-policy establishment. These "wise men" (as the press dubbed them at the time) gathered at Johnson's request and began to discuss the most anguishing of questions: What would it take to defeat the North Vietnamese and the Vietcong once and for all? Would the American people support the mobilization of troops required to gain the initiative? More important, was it time to admit failure and de-escalate the war? After much soul-searching, a consensus was reached: The United States should begin to disengage. Even if victory was possible, a proposition that seemed doubtful, people in the United States were unwilling to make the sacrifices that such a victory might exact. The goal should be to come to terms with Ho Chi Minh. Johnson reluctantly went along with the recommendation.

On March 31, 1968, the president went on national television to announce a halt to the bombing of almost all of North Vietnam. He called upon Hanoi to take this as a positive sign of his willingness to bring an end to the fighting. Recognizing, in effect, that the Vietnam adventure had destroyed his presidency, he also informed the people that he would not seek reelection. Gone were his dreams of leading the country into a new age of social justice and freedom from poverty. The Great Society, Johnson's program for national renewal, died in the jungles of Vietnam. The country was no longer willing to "bear any burden" for the defense of liberty, at least not in South Vietnam.

U.S. combat troops would remain in Southeast Asia until March 1973, but in the aftermath of Tet, it was clear that a turning point had been reached. After March, all talk of victory over the Communists evaporated. The war settled into a stalemate. Casualty lists grew longer and longer, but the situation in the field remained static. Republican Richard Nixon, who won the presidential election of 1968, de-escalated the U.S. military presence gradually, replacing American units with newly trained and equipped South Vietnamese ones. A fragile peace agreement was signed in January 1973, and the last American ground troops left Vietnam quietly in March 1973. From then on, the fighting on the ground was between the ARVN and the Communists. (More on Nixon's handling of the war is discussed in Chapter nine.)

Soon after the last U.S. troops left, the fragile peace agreement broke apart. At first, American air support held off the increasingly strong and aggressive North Vietnamese Army, but in April 1975, South Vietnam fell to the Communists after a lightning-fast invasion by twenty-two divisions of North Vietnamese troops.* America's costly crusade against communism thus ended in abject failure.

The Costs: More than 58,000 Americans lost their lives in the fight. Returning veterans were greeted with derision or ignored by their compatriots. Many, having served a tour of duty after their government no longer

---

*The indigenous military forces, the Vietcong guerrillas, played a progressively smaller role in the war after the Tet Offensive, in part because of their heavy casualties, in part because Hanoi wanted its regular army to exert more control over events. Most of the troops who invaded South Vietnam in 1975 were members of the regular North Vietnamese Army.

sought victory, had become addicted to drugs and alcohol. Perhaps five hundred thousand veterans were suffering (and continue to suffer) from some form of post-traumatic stress disorder, a complicated psychological condition with many symptoms, including nightmares, reliving of combat experiences, and insomnia.

The Vietnam War, the most controversial in the nation's history, had evoked the strongest passions and divided the country in a way that no event had done since the Civil War. The nation's defense posture had been eroded by the drain on resources, and tremendous damage was done to American prestige in the international arena. Ideals died in Vietnam along with a great many—too many—human beings.

In the years following the fall of Saigon, the United States struggled through a deep and long-lasting crisis of confidence, a period of soul-searching over the disastrous turn of events in Southeast Asia and over what role the United States should play in world affairs in the years to come.

Before the war was over, journalists and students of the politics of the United States were well aware that Vietnam had changed the cold war—and many of the ideas that Americans had about communism and their role in combating it. From the late 1960s through the 1970s, the United States showed a decided reluctance to involve itself directly in wars of Communist insurgency. Gone was the exuberant, can-do spirit of the early 1960s that had blinded such men as Kennedy, Bundy, McNamara, and Johnson to the limits of U.S. power, to the tremendous difficulties of fighting an entrenched, well-organized foe—even if the enemy was a so-called third-rate power like North Vietnam. Raw military power and the latest technology did not, it appeared, ensure victory.

One analyst of the failed strategy in Vietnam, an army veteran of that conflict, Colonel Harry Summers, has argued that the military resources of the United States were inappropriately applied by the top decision makers. Summers believes the results in Vietnam might have been different had the U.S. Army concentrated on stopping the flow of troops and supplies into South Vietnam instead of fighting the Vietcong in and around the villages. The United States had more resources and better-trained armed forces than any other nation on earth. But without a proper plan for victory, without the moral support of the people at home, that power could not be properly applied.

In any case, the frustrations of fighting a limited war in Southeast Asia instilled in presidents and in the nation's military leaders a reluctance to use military force unless the objective of the mission was clearly achievable within a measurably short time.

From the beginning of the cold war, the political leaders of the United States had conceived of the struggle against communism in good-versus-evil terms. The moral certitude that lay behind the whole U.S. enterprise in Vietnam—the idea of saving the Vietnamese from the "horrors of Godless communism"—obscured the realities of life and war in Vietnam. It fomented an arrogant confidence in our ability to bring democracy to a people about whose history and culture we were almost completely ignorant. In this sense, Vietnam gave American intervention everywhere a bad name. The adventure in Southeast Asia led many thoughtful people to believe what leftists had been saying for years: that U.S. intervention in the affairs of other nations was motivated more by the interests of the intervener than by a desire to see the peoples of the world determine their own fate.

After 1973, Americans, having been taught a thing or two by the North Vietnamese, developed a greater appreciation for the allure communism held for third world peoples: It promised a way to escape the political and economic chains of old colonial powers such as France and Britain and new or "neocolonial" powers, the most prominent of which, in the eyes of most of the third world, was the United States.

Just as the Americans were realizing that victory in the traditional sense was beyond reach in Vietnam, the experts were announcing some disturbing news: The Soviet Union was reaching or was on the verge of reaching "strategic parity" with the United States in the nuclear arms race. For the first time a Communist country had a nuclear arsenal to equal that of the United States. In the Soviet sphere of influence, there was much to be happy about. History, it was widely believed, was smiling on Moscow and Beijing. The United States' position as leader of the West had been shaken by Vietnam, and there was widespread recognition that the bonds that had formed the Republic and kept it together for almost two hundred years were under the most dire stresses and strains.

In January 1969, that arch anti-Communist, the former Republican vice president of the United States, Richard Milhous Nixon, was inaugurated as the new president. One of the most eventful and surprising eras of the cold war was about to begin.

CHAPTER NINE

FROM NIXON TO CARTER
1969–80

As Richard Nixon took office in January 1969, the United States was unquestionably on the defensive in the cold war. The country was, in fact, in a grim and foul mood. Many observers felt that the atmosphere had not been so foreboding since the days of the Civil War. No fewer than thirty thousand Americans had already died in an increasingly unpopular and morally questionable crusade in Southeast Asia. The growing disillusionment with the war in Vietnam exacerbated other problems.

The war had drained away much-needed money for domestic programs aimed at the poor and the downtrodden in the nation's cities and rural areas. Money to rebuild high-technology defense industries had been siphoned off to pay for the growing war effort. Lavish government spending on Vietnam sparked runaway inflation, which in turn threatened to strip away the savings of millions of hard-working citizens.

Perhaps most ominous was the growing disillusionment felt by young people with traditional American values and institutions, particularly with the U.S. government. By 1969, no one disputed that a youthful and defiant counterculture had blossomed, whose participants were devoted not to a defined political platform as much as to a rejection of their parents' values and outlook. To hundreds of thousands of younger Americans and a good many older ones, the war in Vietnam became a symbol of the moral degeneracy of the establishment (meaning, in effect, the U.S. government and the economic interests that shaped its policies). Leaders of the movement saw the war not as an effort to contain communism but as a venal attempt to expand U.S. power at the expense of a third world nation.

On the other hand, many middle-class Americans found the counterculture's harsh actions and condemnations disturbing. The world as they knew it, in which right had been fairly easy to distinguish from wrong, in which those who were called to serve in the armed forces went willingly and without hesitation, was vanishing before their eyes. People in the United States were frightened and apprehensive.

Richard Nixon had promised to end the war. He claimed to have a plan, but he never revealed the details during the long 1968 presidential campaign. Many observers felt that Nixon owed his election more to his image as a law-and-order man who would be tough on criminals and leftist demonstrators, one who would put an end to violence in the ghettos, than to his promise to end the Vietnam mess. Once in office, however,

President Nixon quickly set about the difficult task of adjusting the country's foreign policies to "new circumstances." The most prominent of these new circumstances were that the nation no longer enjoyed the advantage of clear nuclear and military superiority over the Soviets, and that the American people no longer believed that the United States should be so quick to jump into the role of world policeman.

Nixon's chief accomplishment in the arena of superpower relations was the establishment of détente with the Soviet Union. *Détente,* a French word meaning "the easing of strained relations," did not mean the disappearance of rivalry between the United States and the Soviet Union. It did mean that the world could be a safer place, if for no other reason than that the two countries focused more attention on cooperating than on fighting, on competition than on conflict. Through political summits and economic agreements, arms limitation treaties, and recognition of the Soviet Union as a great power, Nixon hoped to restrain and regulate Soviet behavior in the world. In so doing, he hoped to improve the image and strategic position of the United States.

The task of implementing détente was complicated. For one thing, the president, along with his national security adviser, Henry Kissinger, had to deal with a Soviet Union that had been developing and building new weapons systems at a breakneck pace. By that time, the Soviet Union had at its disposal about twelve hundred ICBMs, slightly more than the United States had. The Soviet navy was emerging as a rival to that of the

United States. It had developed Polaris-like nuclear missiles for its submarines. The new, improved Soviet fleet was a great worry for American strategists: For the first time, the Soviet Union was capable of projecting its forces beyond Europe and Asia.

And then, of course, there was the key factor of increased Soviet confidence: Its military machine was now much more formidable than it had been in the days of the Cuban Missile Crisis. Many experts felt it was the equal of its rival's forces. Certainly Premier Leonid Brezhnev was determined to make one thing perfectly clear: His nation had armed forces every bit as deadly as those of the United States. He had only recently (August 1968) crushed a reform movement in Czechoslovakia, sending in Soviet tanks, and then announced what became known as the Brezhnev Doctrine: the right of the Soviet Union to intervene when Communist governments were threatened—anywhere. (The invasion of Czechoslovakia only confirmed Washington's impression that the Soviets were entering a new, more aggressive foreign-policy phase.)

The challenges were great. To his credit, Richard Nixon kept a cool head and focused his energies on the opportunities instead of on the obstacles. The war in Vietnam could be, must be, ended, without destroying U.S. leadership of the free world. For all its new strength, the Soviet Union faced grave economic adversity. It needed Western technological assistance and would therefore be receptive to bargaining. Nixon recognized that he still had good cards to play, despite setbacks in Vietnam and elsewhere in the third world, where the Soviet drive to gain friends had been more successful than Washington liked.

At the core of détente was the possibility of a new kind of relationship with the Soviets. It had to be rooted in carefully worded, very specific agreements, not the kind of "we agree on the following democratic principles" approach that had failed the West at Yalta and had led to such great disillusionment in the United States and Western Europe. For the plain fact was that when it came to interpreting the meaning of words like *freedom* and *democracy*, there was no common ground between West and East. Nixon's recognition of this was a clear indication of the faith he placed in the idea of *Realpolitik*, a school of political thought that holds that relations between nations ought be based on practical solutions and upon a candid assessment of differences in interests rather than on theoretical or ethical objectives.

One aspect of the rivalry desperately in need of concrete, specific agreements was that of nuclear arms. The new president resolved, if not to halt the increasingly expensive buildup of these weapons, at least to open channels of discussion with a view to limiting future expenditures. Procedures needed to be established to prevent a war that could conceivably put an end to humanity. Both sides had great incentives to accomplish arms limitations.

The chief architect of Nixon's innovative foreign policy was his national security adviser and, later, secretary of state, Professor Henry Kissinger of Harvard. A Jewish refugee from Hitler's Germany, Kissinger had had an impressive career as a scholar and teacher before entering government service. Despite the vast differences in backgrounds, Nixon and Kissinger shared certain convictions concerning the cold war and how it had been conducted.

United States strategy in the recent past had too often been shaped by short-term considerations and by the naive belief that any gain for the Russians in world affairs was a loss for the United States. In an age when two great powers had huge nuclear arsenals, the United States needed to take a longer-term, more discriminating view of the world and its dangers. The United States had limited resources; it was not capable of remaking the world in its own image as so many in government had once believed it was. Nor could it possibly respond to every Communist insurgency that cropped up in the world. To do so would result only in exhaustion, demoralization, and failure. Like Nixon, Kissinger held that U.S. defense commitments had grown beyond the nation's capacity to support them.

Kissinger had a great deal of faith in the traditional ideas that had governed great-power relations among European countries in the eighteenth and nineteenth centuries. The most important of these was the balance of power, the notion that stability could best be achieved by the presence of several strong powers that could, in effect, offset one another's aggressive tendencies. In the international arena, Nixon and Kissinger sought stability and order rather than American dominance.

Both men believed that stability was best achieved when foreign policy was made by the few; hence they sought, with much success, to limit as much as possible the role of Congress in making critical foreign-policy decisions. In this way, the administration had a free hand to bargain and maneuver as it saw fit. With this approach to making foreign-policy decisions, they began to address the problem of restoring the balance of power in a vexing trouble spot: Vietnam.

Nixon and Kissinger were fully aware that real victory in Vietnam was beyond reach. Nonetheless, they realized the horrendous price the United States would pay if it suddenly pulled up stakes and ran, leaving South Vietnam to almost certain collapse. Such a move would have disintegrated the American nation's credibility in the eyes of allies; equally important, it would have signaled a lack of resolve to the Chinese and the Soviets. It would also have spelled the end for Nixon and Kissinger's plan for a more stable balance of power in world politics. So began the long pursuit of what the president termed "peace with honor" in Vietnam.

Part of the master plan developed by the Nixon administration for ending the war in Indochina was the policy of "Vietnamization." South Vietnamese troops would carry an increasingly larger share of the fighting as U.S. ground forces were gradually withdrawn. At the same time the United States undertook, through various aid packages, to shore up South Vietnam's economy and its army. (In 1973 *alone*, Nixon would send South Vietnam $3.2 billion worth of arms.)

In November 1969, the president called upon the American people, in his "silent majority" speech, to stand by his plan for an honorable exit from Vietnam. At the same time Nixon sought, through the offering of various economic and diplomatic incentives, to enlist the aid of Communist China and the USSR in his effort to end the war on the most favorable terms possible for the United States. In effect, he and Kissinger said to Beijing and Moscow, "Good things are in the offing if you help us out of this jam by applying pressure on the North Vietnamese to bring an end to the fighting on terms that do not humiliate the United States."

During the first year of the new administration, the plan appeared to work. Criticism of the war effort tailed off. To increase pressure on the North Vietnamese at the negotiating table, the president ordered the secret bombing of Communist staging and supply areas in Cambodia in March 1969. A year later, as Communist forces sought to take advantage of a coup in Phnom Penh, Cambodia's capital, Nixon again demonstrated his determination to punish the North Vietnamese by invading Cambodia and destroying huge quantities of supplies.

The Cambodian "incursion" set off a firestorm of protest in the United States. Four students were shot and killed by jittery National Guardsmen during one such protest at Kent State University in Ohio, sparking a new chorus of voices calling on Nixon to end the war. But Nixon and Kissinger, believing that a quick with-drawal would have a disastrous impact on their plans to reconfigure the world balance of power through détente, would have none of it. "We will not be humili-ated. We will not be defeated," Nixon told the American people in April 1970. "If when the chips are down the U.S. acts like a pitiful helpless giant, the forces of totalitarianism and anarchy will threaten free nations and free institutions throughout the world."[1]

Fighting continued throughout 1971. For their part, the North Vietnamese showed little flexibility; they clung tenaciously to their goal of unifying the country under Hanoi. The official position put forward at the negotiations in Paris was that Hanoi wanted a peace agreement establishing a coalition, or multifaction, government for all South Vietnam, in which it would play a central part. The North Vietnamese demanded in addition that President Thieu of South Vietnam step down. This seemed a ruse to Washington, and it was abruptly refused. Nixon and Kissinger continued to insist that all North Vietnamese troops leave South Vietnamese soil before an agreement could be reached.

In April 1972, the NVA launched the first of its two attempts to avoid all negotiations and take South Vietnam by force of arms. The Eastertide Offensive, a massive, three-pronged attack with tanks and 120,000 troops, overwhelmed many ARVN units and was brought to a screeching halt only when Nixon, furious that the North Vietnamese were trying to take advantage of U.S. troop withdrawals—only about 70,000 American troops remained in-country—ordered B-52 attacks and unleashed fighter-bombers from no fewer than six aircraft carriers. The air strikes proved effective, driving the NVA back into Cambodia, and left North Vietnam with heavy losses. Hanoi, as well as its major port, Haiphong, were also bombed. Nixon ordered the mining of Haiphong harbor and a blockade of North Vietnam.

Negotiations continued. So did the fighting. In

October 1972, it appeared for a while that a cease-fire had been brokered. The North Vietnamese dropped the demand for the ouster of Thieu; the United States no longer demanded the complete removal of NVA units from South Vietnamese territory. But the various parties (in addition to the North Vietnamese and the Americans, there were representatives from the Thieu government and the Vietcong, the politico-military organization in South Vietnam that took orders from Hanoi) bogged down in the details. When the talks broke down once more, Nixon again unleashed the U.S. Air Force against targets in and around Hanoi and Haiphong. This, coupled with subtle signs sent to Hanoi by Beijing and Moscow that it would be best to end the war sooner rather than later, led to resumed negotiations.

In January 1973, the parties finally reached an agreement. The terms were essentially those reached a year earlier, except now it was agreed not to discuss South Vietnam's permanent political future at all. That would have to be settled later. No party, the agreement stated, would attempt to expand the amount of South Vietnamese territory under its control at the date of signing. The United States would withdraw all its troops by March 1973, and North Vietnam would return all prisoners of war.

Under the circumstances—North Vietnam clearly had a great deal of military leverage with its troops well established in South Vietnam—it was about the best the United States could have expected. It would leave Vietnam with the current South Vietnamese government still in power.

Why, it might be asked, did Nixon press on with the war for so long when so many in America wanted it to end? Later Nixon himself provided an answer: "The way in which the United States met its responsibilities in Vietnam [would] be crucial to the Soviet and Chinese assessment of American will, and thus to the success of any new relationship with those powers."[2]

South Vietnam did, of course, fall to the Communists two years later, a clear defeat for the United States. By that time, however, Nixon had limited the damage of American failure in Vietnam by opening up constructive diplomatic relations with the governments of the People's Republic of China and the Soviet Union. It is to these stories that we now turn.

China had been involved in bitter border skirmishes with Soviet troops since March 1969. Long before that, the two countries had begun to squabble about the best ways to deal with the West and how best to support Communist insurgencies in the third world. Beijing had often been critical of the Soviets for being too concilia-tory toward the United States and its allies, especially during the Khrushchev era. For their part the Soviets felt the Chinese were altogether too quick to challenge Moscow's leadership of international communism. So it was that ideological brotherhood slipped into another rivalry between two great powers. Furthermore, as early as 1960, the USSR had stopped giving China military and economic assistance. China had become a nuclear power, testing its first A-bomb in 1964 and its first H-bomb in 1967, without Soviet help.

Kissinger and Nixon saw an opportunity to enlist China in what had been the major American objective in the cold war: the containment of Soviet power. This occurred at a time when many experts thought that Brezhnev was pressing to achieve outright military superiority over the United States. (The Soviets had recently sent planes and surface-to-air missiles to Egypt in great numbers. In late 1970, the Kremlin built a new submarine base in Cuba, violating the 1962 agreement reached after the Cuban Missile Crisis.)

Good relations with China did not emerge overnight. The United States had virtually no contact with China's leader, the hero of the 1949 revolution, Mao Zedong. The "loss" of China in 1949 to Communists had come as a terrible blow to policy makers in Washington early in the cold war. That had soon been followed by the outbreak of war in Korea, which pitted the United States directly against China.

Since that time, the relationship had been characterized by unremitting hostility. The United States successfully blocked Communist China from admittance to the United Nations until 1971. Nixon himself had the reputation of a hard-liner when it came to the Communists on mainland China; but he turned this to his advantage in forging the new relationship. Political rivals would have a difficult time accusing him of being "soft" on the Chinese Communists.

The warming-up process started with a few polite inquiries through diplomatic channels concerning improvement of relations. Mao, too, seemed interested in a change. In April 1971 an invitation came for an

American team to participate in a table-tennis (Ping-Pong) tournament. Mao told the American journalist Edgar Snow that he "would be happy to talk with [Nixon] either as a tourist or as a President."[3]

The groundwork for Nixon's historic February 1972 trip to China was laid by Kissinger, with the help of the Pakistanis. It was done (in typical Kissinger style) under a shroud of secrecy. In the summer of 1971, while Kissinger was in Pakistan, carefully planned news reports surfaced that he was ill and would not be following his itinerary. In fact, he was whisked away to an airport and flown to China to meet with high-level Chinese officials. The U.S. national security adviser explained the administration's new attitude toward China to Zhou Enlai, at the time China's second most powerful political figure. According to the Nixon administration, the international community needed a more stable balance of power in the world as a whole. A better relationship between the United States and China would enhance world stability and act as a needed check on Soviet expansionism. Zhou Enlai was receptive. He was well aware that China could benefit greatly from better trade relations with the United States and the West. And improved relations would give China additional leverage in dealing with the Soviet Union, with which China was having myriad problems, including fighting along their common border.

The major stumbling block, as the Chinese saw it, was the United States' continued political and financial support for the Nationalist Chinese government on Taiwan (formerly called Formosa). Kissinger indicated that something could be done about that, and it was.

The United States announced in August that it would support the seating of the People's Republic of China in the UN but that it remained committed to protecting the security of the Nationalist Chinese on the island of Taiwan. Kissinger's statement appeared to satisfy Beijing. (In October 1971 the United Nations seated the People's Republic of China and expelled Nationalist China.)

Nixon's trip to China greatly enhanced his standing as a statesman. The presidential entourage arrived in the ancient capital of Beijing in February 1972 and was welcomed with much fanfare. The ten-day stay was replete with surprising images that fitted such an occasion, including that of Nixon, the hard-line anti-Communist, happily dining with Mao and using chopsticks. No important agreements were reached; no one expected any. The joint statement issued at the end of the trip indicated that the two sides agreed on general rules of international relations. Both sides also acknowledged that the normalization of relations between the two giants was "in the interests of all nations." The two nations would expand their trading activities. The cold war, at least so far as China was concerned, seemed to be melting away.

Well before Nixon had made his historic trek to China, the serious work of altering the relationship with Moscow had begun. The focus was on limiting nuclear weapons. The Strategic Arms Limitation Talks (SALT) began in the fall of 1969 in Helsinki, Finland, and continued with various ups and downs for about three years. Both Washington and Moscow realized the benefits of limiting nuclear arms. It saved money, billions of dollars by most estimates. It made both governments appear to be responsible in the eyes of the community of nations. But there was a more profound and pressing reason: nuclear instability.

The basic idea behind U.S. nuclear strategy was, in the parlance of the experts, "mutually assured destruction." The idea was that both sides were prevented from launching an attack by the knowledge that the first attack by one side would surely lead to the devastation of both sides. By the late 1960s, the proliferation of different types of nuclear weapons threatened to throw off this delicate balance. Both the United States and the Soviet Union were planning to add antiballistic missile (ABM) systems—that is, missiles designed to shoot down other missiles—to their inventory. In addition, the Russians now had a supply of missiles to be launched from the sea. The United States developed a completely new offensive weapon, the multiple independently targeted reentry vehicle (MIRV), a missile that could shoot two or more separate nuclear warheads at different targets with one press of the button. These new weapons, more complicated and varied than those of the previous generation, made the nasty business of predicting what might happen if there was some altercation between the superpowers far more difficult than it had been.

After several years of sorting through the morass of assumptions and counterassumptions about the interplay between offensive and defensive weapons, the parties announced in May 1971 that they had agreed, in principle, to the first nuclear arms limitation agreement of the cold war. Over the next eleven months, Henry Kissinger and his negotiating team worked out an elaborately detailed agreement with his highly capable counterpart, Soviet Foreign Minister Andrei Gromyko.

At the end of a much-publicized presidential trip to Moscow, Brezhnev and Nixon signed the formal SALT I agreement, which froze for five years the number of ICBMs and submarine-launched ballistic missiles deployed or under construction as of May 1972 in each country's arsenal. SALT I also placed strict limits on the development of antiballistic missile systems. Neither country could establish a nationwide system to fend off an attack, and only two ABM sites could be set up in each country. The United States at the time had no operational defensive missiles (ABMs), while the Russians had only a small system in place.

This part of the agreement was designed to ensure that no elaborate, all-encompassing defensive systems would be emplaced and thus give one side a "first-strike" capability without incurring great risk of retaliation. As Nixon explained years later in his memoirs, "By giving up missile defense, each side was leaving its population hostage to a strategic missile attack. Each side therefore had an ultimate interest in preventing a war that could only be mutually destructive."[4]

The United States possessed some eighteen hundred missiles of these types, the Soviets about twenty-six hundred. It was argued by the treaty's defenders that the gap was more than equalized by the fact that the United States had MIRVs; that is, it could send more warheads toward Soviet targets than the Russians could send toward Western targets. In almost every category, American missiles were more accurate.

The two parties also agreed not to interfere with each other's reconnaissance efforts, conducted largely by space satellite, to verify whether the terms of the treaty were kept.

Critics of the SALT I agreement point out that it did not stop the arms race. While a number of categories of weapons had been restricted quantitatively, the door was left open for both sides to improve the quality of those weapons (and thus throw the delicate balance out of whack once again). No limit was placed on either side's arsenal of nuclear warheads. Mistrust and doubt remained salient features in the relationship, and both parties continued to build warheads in great numbers. In 1973 the United States had 6,000 warheads, the Soviets 2,500. By 1977, the numbers had changed to 10,000 and 4,000 respectively.

Nevertheless, SALT I was a profound accomplishment. It injected a long-overdue measure of hope into the U.S.-Soviet rivalry. "The offensive freeze," observed one student of the subject,

> was intended to give [the superpowers] time to negotiate a more lasting agreement. SALT I was to be the beginning of a process, a continuing dialogue and effort to control the arms competition. The two nuclear giants appeared to recognize their special obligation for the preservation of peace by complementing SALT I with certain standards of behavior. They pledged to avoid confrontations, to exercise

mutual restraint, and to reject efforts to gain unilateral advantages.[5]

SALT I ushered in the sunniest period in U.S.–USSR
relations since the days of the World War II alliance. A
spate of agreements followed: The two nations agreed to
plan a joint mission in space for 1975, to a huge purchase of U.S. wheat by the Soviets, and to more trade.
The scientific communities of the two powers agreed to
share information about the oceans and pollution and
even some advanced technology projects. Leonid
Brezhnev, in Washington for a June 1973 summit with
President Nixon, was treated as an old friend. At one
point in the festivities, the burly Soviet leader even
announced that the cold war was over.

The announcement was perhaps premature, but the
statesmen were clearly moving in a positive direction.
They agreed to tackle one of the trickier issues upon
which they held vastly differing views: the levels of conventional forces—soldiers with rifles, tanks, and nonnuclear airpower—in Europe.

Détente owed its existence, in part, to the ingenuity,
dexterity, and willpower of Nixon, Kissinger, and their
support staffs. But there was a dark side to their quest
for stability and order. Both the president and Kissinger,
appointed secretary of state in 1973, were disdainful of
bureaucracy, of trying to run policy through the officially prescribed chain of governmental offices and procedures. The two had conspired, with great success, to
keep the State Department and Congress out of foreign-
policy decisions. They shared a deep mistrust of com-

mittees and power sharing, especially with a Democratic Congress overburdened with "dovish" Democrats, who lacked the stomach for playing the *Realpolitik* game.

As the voices grew louder in protest over U.S. policy in Vietnam and what the critics saw as the U.S. government's de-emphasis of human rights as a guiding principle in shaping its relations with other nations (notably Chile and Iran), the Nixon administration went about squelching dissent and indulging in a wide variety of unethical, and in many cases illegal, activities. Most of these acts were aimed at discrediting the administration's political adversaries in the United States. Although it remains unclear exactly which illegal acts the president himself authorized, it is certain that Nixon gave his blessings to the vicious smear and intimidation campaign carried out by his underlings during 1972 and 1973 against key figures in the antiwar movement, potential Democratic rivals, and other nay-sayers. The arrogance of it all was captured by one of Kissinger's cynical remarks: "The illegal we do immediately; the unconstitutional takes a little longer."[6]

As it happened, "a little longer" was all the time Mr. Nixon had. By mid-1973, Congress had opened hearings on the infamous Watergate break-ins, in which the Committee to Re-elect the President had burglarized the headquarters of the Democratic Party. It was not long after the hearings began, under the judicious guidance of Senator Sam Ervin of North Carolina, that Nixon himself was implicated in illegal wiretappings, the burglary, and even the misuse of campaign funds. It was a demoralizing period for the American people.

Nixon, as one might have guessed, was not one to quit easily—he thrived on conflict—and he counterattacked with stubborn ferocity. Yes, the president explained, he may have committed indiscretions, but if he had, it had been in the best interests of the American people at a crucial time. He was not a liar. He was not a crook. This line of argument, however, appeared unconvincing to both Washington officialdom and to the public, who observed the Watergate hearings on television with intense interest.

Nixon's abuse of the presidency, coupled with the failure of the crusade in Vietnam orchestrated by various presidents, led to a congressional backlash against what pundits now called "the Imperial Presidency." In July 1973, the Fulbright-Aiken Amendment prohibited newly appropriated funds from being expended "to finance directly or indirectly combat activities by the U.S. military forces in or over or from the shores of North Vietnam, South Vietnam, Laos or Cambodia."[7] Congress had successfully invoked the power of the purse to send the president an unambiguous message: Further adventures in Indochina would not be tolerated. In November, the War Powers Act, which stipulated that the president must consult with Congress "in every possible instance" before sending troops into a potentially hostile situation, passed into law over Nixon's veto.

While Congress was putting the finishing touches on the final version of the War Powers Act in October 1973, it appeared that U.S. forces might be sent to another part of the globe. This time the trouble was in the Middle East. The Egyptians, allies of the Soviets, were smarting from defeat at the hands of the well trained and highly motivated Israelis, whose staunchest ally was the United States. In October Egypt attacked Israeli positions in the lands occupied during the 1967 war. The Israelis, caught by surprise, were driven back.

The United States undertook a costly and rapid airlift to supply the Israeli army, which managed to halt the advancing Egyptians. The Israelis then attempted a daring and successful counterattack. Three weeks into the Yom Kippur War, a large army of Egyptians found itself surrounded and on the verge of being entirely destroyed. Now the Soviets readied an airlift. The old fears of a permanent Soviet military presence in the oil-rich Middle East arose once again in Washington. Fear turned to outright alarm upon receipt of a CIA report indicating that the Soviets had seven USSR divisions—more than one hundred thousand men—ready to be moved to the Middle East.

On Kissinger's advice, Nixon sent a sternly worded message to Moscow. The United States would not stand idly by while the Soviets took advantage of a bad situation. Nixon also put U.S. armed forces around the world on alert, including SAC, the Strategic Air Command. All of this apparently shook Brezhnev, for he soon agreed to the deployment of a UN-sponsored peacekeeping force of nonnuclear powers to disengage the troops. Having dispensed with the immediate threat of a direct superpower confrontation, Nixon and Kissinger began to engineer a peace plan that, however imperfect and incomplete, put an end to the Yom Kippur War and one chapter in the stormy relationship between Israel and its Arab neighbors.

In the summer of 1974, Nixon the statesman was on the move. A trip to Egypt in June was followed by one to Moscow in July, during which the American president, beset by increasingly ominous revelations of misconduct at home, signed a limited nuclear test-ban treaty. On August 8, 1974, facing impeachment and possible criminal charges, Richard Milhous Nixon announced his resignation (to go into effect the next day) from the office of president of the United States.

With Richard Nixon's departure from the White House, Vice-President Gerald R. Ford—an amiable former congressman from Michigan whom Nixon had appointed to the second-in-command post after Vice-President Spiro T. Agnew was forced to resign under a cloud in October 1973—became president. Unlike his predecessor, Ford had little inclination for mastering the intricacies of foreign policy. He sought no radical changes in relations with the Soviets; nor did he have any particularly inventive ideas on how to cope with communism in the third world.

Ford pardoned his former boss in September 1974, thereby ensuring that the world would not witness the humiliating spectacle of an American president on trial in a criminal court. Kissinger, who had not been implicated in Watergate, stayed on as secretary of state under Ford.

The new president's first run-in with a Communist regime showed that he, like Nixon, had no intention of letting lesser powers take advantage of recent American setbacks. When the Cambodian navy claimed that the freighter *Mayagüez* (which sailed under a U.S. flag) was in its waters and seized the ship, Ford sent the U.S. Marines into Cambodia to rescue the crew. They succeeded, although they sustained heavy casualties in the process.

The *Mayagüez* incident, which unfolded just a few weeks after the humiliating evacuation of Americans from Saigon in April 1975, boosted morale at home. But a wary Congress, reflecting the increasingly isolationist sentiments of the people, proved in the ensuing months to have little stomach for United States intervention in cold war hot spots.

This was made clear in the summer of 1975, when the Portuguese colony of Angola, in Africa, exploded into civil war. One of the factions in that bitter struggle was the Popular Movement for the Liberation of Angola. It was Marxist in outlook and had enjoyed extensive support from Moscow. When fifteen thousand highly trained Cuban regulars appeared in Angola, the CIA sought funds for covert operations to check the gains of the Soviet-supported faction. The House of Representatives refused to grant money. Here and elsewhere, the American people, through their elected leaders, appeared to be telling the foreign-policy decision makers that it was time to scale back U.S. commitments abroad.

Gerald Ford's most significant act as a cold war statesman and purveyor of détente was his signing of the Helsinki Accords at a "supersummit" in 1975. The meeting in neutral Finland featured heads of state from every European country with the exception of Albania. Leonid Brezhnev was also in attendance. At Helsinki, the parties agreed to respect all existing European borders as permanent, thereby *formally* accepting, for the first time, Soviet political dominance of Eastern Europe. There was something of a victory in convincing the Soviet Union to agree to the principle of "nonintervention in the internal affairs" of any other state. The Brezhnev Doctrine of 1968 (invoked against Czechoslovakia) had held that the USSR had a right to intervene in the affairs of any Communist regime. Finally, the accords called for greater respect for human rights throughout the world.

Helsinki indicated that détente was working, in that the Soviet Union, by entering into these agreements, seemed to have put aside its theoretical, revolutionary goal of turning the world into one great Communist camp. It signaled a more open and candid relationship between East and West. Nevertheless, the voices of criticism in the United States, speaking against détente and the outlook of the men who fashioned it, were heard with increased frequency in the mid-1970s.

The most damning charge against détente was that it had removed the moral underpinning from U.S. foreign policy. The authority of America's leadership had long been rooted in the idea of carrying freedom and democratic values to distant shores. Détente dispensed with that; what mattered was the balance of power, not the treatment of peoples. Hence it was acceptable, even at times desirable (in Nixon's and Kissinger's view), for the United States to favor nations that occupied strategically important locations. What if those nations had governments that abused their people? Well . . . that was unfortunate, but certainly not worth a reversal of U.S. policy.

Left-of-center critics began to paint a portrait of the now disgraced Nixon and his right-hand man, Kissinger, as morally bankrupt manipulators, as opportunists with no more interest in extending freedom than their archrivals in the Kremlin. Kissinger considered his critics naive: To think one could effect change in Communist states by attacking and embarrassing them for their human rights abuses was, in his view, absurd. It would only anger the Soviets to such a point that agreements on important things such as nuclear weapons and multinational trade treaties would become impossible.

Criticism of détente, a crisis of confidence over the United States' mission in the world after Vietnam, and a general dissatisfaction with Washington opened the door for the election of James Earl Carter to the presidency in November 1976. The former governor of Georgia, a Democrat who thought of himself as a Washington "outsider," hoped to restore moral integrity to his office, to heal the nation's wounds, and to rebuild confidence in the country as the leader of the free world.

Jimmy Carter was by all accounts hardworking, idealistic, and intelligent. Unfortunately, he was inexperienced in the wheeling and dealing ways of Congress. He was unfamiliar with the intricacies of international politics. Carter was also a bit unlucky and not quite sure how to go about reaching his objectives. All of this spelled trouble for détente.

The new president appointed some impressive

people, including Cyrus R. Vance as his secretary of state and Harold Brown as the head of the Defense Department, both old Washington hands with a reputation for getting things done. Not long into his term, however, insiders were saying that the executive branch as a whole was in disarray. "Division plagued the administration from the start," wrote Robert Divine in his *Politics and Diplomacy in Recent American History.* "The most serious conflict of all developed over the formulation and conduct of foreign policy."[8]

The foreign-policy debate centered on the rivalry between Vance and the national security adviser, Zbigniew Brzezinski. These men had very different ideas on many things, including how to handle the Russians. Brzezinski, a staunch anti-Communist born and raised in Poland, feared the Soviets were on a third world offensive; he thought the proper approach was to initiate a buildup of U.S. forces to deter Soviet adventurism. Vance wanted to downplay conflict with the Soviet Union and at the same time expand connections with the third world.

Carter's early pronouncements on foreign policy seemed to favor the Vance approach. He wanted to reinvigorate U.S. policy by putting a new emphasis on moral leadership. The United States, Carter informed the people, would treat nations that respected human rights as friends; those governments with records of repression would be held at arm's length. Only when their records showed marked improvement would they be eligible for economic and social aid. In short, Carter thought "the demonstration of American idealism was a practical and realistic approach to foreign affairs and moral principles were the best foundation for the exertion of American power and influence."[9]

The president acted on his beliefs. Early in 1977, he openly encouraged Soviet dissident intellectuals, who were demanding that the government allow freedom of expression. Brezhnev was livid. He read Carter's action as a deliberate attempt to embarrass Moscow and as interference in the internal affairs of his country. The Kremlin took notice, too, that Carter tended to downplay abuses in countries, such as South Korea, of strategic significance to the United States.

Carter's attempts to move détente forward on other fronts also fell flat. Soon after assuming office, the president started in a positive way by announcing that he planned to order the withdrawal of nuclear weapons from South Korea. (In fact, the South Koreans did not confirm that all U.S. nuclear weapons were removed from their soil until the early 1990s.) He hoped at the very least for a positive response from Moscow. None came. On the contrary, the Soviets seemed to interpret Carter's action as a sign of weakness. The USSR pressed forward energetically with an arms buildup and began to support a pro-Marxist faction in the African nation of Ethiopia.

When nuclear arms control talks resumed in Moscow in March 1977, Carter proposed deeper cuts in ICBMs than had been envisioned by either Ford or Brezhnev. The proposal was rebuffed by the Soviet team as being one-sided, a deliberate attempt to undermine the earlier understandings worked out by Ford, Gromyko, and Brezhnev. Foreign Minister Gromyko went so far as to call the proposal a "cheap and shady maneuver"—

strong language from an experienced diplomat.[10]

Carter's one triumph in arms control was the signing of the SALT II agreement with Leonid Brezhnev in Vienna in June 1979. The treaty, worked out largely by Vance, placed a two-year delay on the deployment of American cruise missiles (highly effective low-flying rockets with nuclear warheads), but it did permit the United States to modernize its submarine-based missiles and to develop a less vulnerable ICBM system, the MX, with missiles that could be quickly moved to avoid becoming easy targets.

SALT II drew a great deal of flak in the United States. The critics said Jimmy Carter was giving away America's edge in the strategic rivalry, that he was soft on communism generally. Carter began to take a tougher line with the Soviets, at least in his speeches. The Russians, for their part, found it hard to know what the president really wanted.

In the volatile Middle East, too, there were developments that boded poorly for the United States. After years of conflict with America's most important ally in the region, Israel, the nations of Syria, Libya, and Iraq all sought closer relationships with the Kremlin. In Southeast Asia, vacated U.S. military bases were occupied by Russian forces, and a treaty of friendship between the Soviet Union and Vietnam was signed.

The nation faced another serious strategic setback in late 1979 when the repressive shah of Iran, Mohammad Reza Pahlavi, a longtime U.S. ally but despised by most Iranians, was overthrown by Islamic fundamentalists led by Ayatollah Ruhollah Khomeini. When President Carter let the deposed monarch into the United States for medical treatment, the U.S. embassy in Tehran was attacked by about four hundred angry radicals, many of them students. In a move unprecedented in modern history, the government of Iran applauded the radicals when they seized the occupants of the embassy as hostages in November and began a long and daunting campaign—some 444 days—of lectures and public spectacles designed to humiliate Carter and the United States.

The president approved a rescue mission in which U.S. commandos were to break into the embassy. It came to a bad end when three helicopters were caught in a giant sandstorm and crashed in the desert, killing eight servicemen. The hostage affair consumed Carter; at times he seemed to care about little else. To many around the world and in the United States, it symbolized Carter's ineffectiveness as a leader.

Only six weeks after the Americans had been seized in Iran, and six months after the United States and the Soviet Union had signed a second SALT agreement placing further limitations on nuclear weapons, the Soviet Union invaded its mountainous neighbor Afghanistan. The Kremlin claimed the intervention was necessary to crush a Muslim uprising against the Communist government then in power. By the beginning of the new year, fifty thousand Soviet soldiers were in Afghanistan. It was to become the Soviet Union's Vietnam.

The invasion shocked Washington. The Red Army was on the march; for the first time since the end of World War II, it was operating outside the territory taken from Hitler. Carter reported to the American people that "the implications of the Soviet invasion of Afghanistan could pose the most serious threat to world peace since the Second World War."[11] In protest, Carter withdrew the SALT II treaty from the Senate's consideration and began to take a very tough line with the Soviets. He embargoed the sale of high-technology equipment to the Soviet Union and reinstituted military draft registration in the United States. He planned to increase defense spending to meet the new challenge. He withdrew the U.S. Olympic Team from the summer games in Moscow.

All of this had little effect on the Russians. For the Americans the failure to prevent the Soviet invasion of Afghanistan seemed one more incident in a long series of frustrations. Carter's apparent impotence in Iran, his vacillation and inability to devise a coherent strategy for dealing with Soviet adventurism in the third world, and a troubled economy all contributed to the Georgian's political decline. In November 1980 he was trounced in the presidential election by the former governor of California, Ronald Wilson Reagan. Reagan promised to renew America's self-confidence and to stand up to the Russians. He did exactly that—among other things.

CHAPTER TEN

THE 1980s:
COLD WAR II AND
THE END OF AN ERA

The 1980s was a decade of contrasts and changes. With Ronald Reagan's ascent to the presidency, relations with the Soviet Union took a grim turn. Reagan had been elected, in part, because he promised to talk—and act—tough to the Soviets. The cold war had always been a complicated tapestry of military competition, political conflict, propaganda, and diplomatic maneuvering. In the early 1980s the emphasis, in both Washington and Moscow, was on conflict.

Each side made some unusually ominous pronouncements about its rival. It was widely believed that the leaders of both countries were acting recklessly, that they were almost looking for an excuse to go at one another. With the mid-1980s came new and more open-minded leadership in the Kremlin, a new attitude in Washington, and the thawing of the superpower relationship.

Once the new Soviet general secretary of the Communist Party, Mikhail Gorbachev, made or was forced into making a firm commitment to change (circa 1986), a series of startling developments followed: the withering away of suspicion and mistrust; the emergence of a refreshing spirit of cooperation, even friendship, between the leaders of the superpowers; the rapid breakdown of totalitarian control in Eastern Europe; and amazingly, the collapse of communism in the USSR itself. By the decade's end, and for the first time in forty-five years, the Soviet–American rivalry was no longer the dominant story in international politics. Pundits on the Right and Left proclaimed that a "new world order" was in the making. There was much rejoicing, but also much uncertainty about the shape of the future.

The president of the United States through most of the decade was a man with strong ideas about the evils of communism and an abiding faith in the wonders of democracy and the American people. Or so it appeared to many in the United States.

Ronald Reagan began his working life as a radio sportscaster in the Midwest. In the 1940s and 1950s he appeared in starring roles in a number of Hollywood B movies, many of them Westerns. That led to other opportunities. He achieved some celebrity as a public relations spokesman for General Electric, touring the country and giving talks on the virtues of small government and free enterprise. Then Reagan entered politics. He was elected to the governorship of California in 1966 and served two terms, becoming a figure to be reckoned with among conservatives.

The fortieth U.S. president was a likable man, with an infectious smile and a touch, it was often said, of the common man. His critics, though, said he approached the presidency as if it were another acting role. There was at least a kernel of truth to their claims. More than any other president in history, Reagan depended on prepared scripts. He had certain convictions and preoccupations but appeared to know (and read) little about political and social issues. He didn't have a good memory for detail and was often confused about what position his administration had put forward on any given issue—whether it concerned a negotiating position on ICBMs or whom we were trying to defeat or defend in Central America. Talking off the cuff tended to land him in trouble, and so his aides went to great lengths to limit the president's opportunities for spontaneous responses to reporters' questions. After he had left office, Reagan's national security adviser, Robert MacFarlane, remarked that while he was on staff in the White House, the amiable president couldn't always remember his adviser's name.

Despite these limitations, Ronald Reagan was a very popular president. "He had learned how to play the role of the wholesome American who would set things right," observed the biographer Lou Cannon. "Because of his ability to reflect and give voice to the aspirations of his fellow citizens, Reagan succeeded in reviving national confidence when there was a great need for inspiration."[1]

The Reagan message for Americans was that their

day in the sun lay in the future, not the past. Yes, the nation had experienced setbacks and tragedies. But there was no need, Reagan told the people, for further hand-wringing and self-doubt. Vietnam had been a noble cause gone wrong. The United States of America was still the greatest country on earth. Its citizens were the envy of peoples around the world and, perhaps most significantly, still the leaders of the free world in the struggle against the "evil empire," the USSR.

Foreign policy was to play a critical role in the enormous confidence-building job that lay ahead. The Reagan plan, formed in close consultation with a tough-minded cabinet led by Caspar W. Weinberger at Defense and Alexander M. Haig, Jr., at State, was designed to seize the initiative from the Soviets.

No question about it, the Reagan team reasoned, communism had made inroads in Central America, taking shrewd advantage of the poverty and social unrest that pervaded the Western Hemisphere south of the United States. In nuclear weapons, the Soviet Union had gained "strategic parity"; that is, it was roughly equal to the United States in numbers of missiles and the like. The Kremlin had sought to take advantage of the American public's reluctance to involve the nation in foreign entanglements and had thus stepped up its efforts in the third world to win power for Marxist factions in Angola, Ethiopia, Afghanistan, Nicaragua, and Peru.

How was the initiative to be seized? Recognizing that perception and belief were vital factors in the super-power rivalry, President Reagan stepped up the war of words between East and West. In pronouncement after pronouncement, he sought to drum up patriotic fervor. The United States was the beacon of hope for oppressed peoples everywhere; the Soviet Union was an "evil empire," the "focus of evil" in the modern world. At his first press conference as president in 1981, Reagan went so far as to accuse the Kremlin leaders of "reserving unto themselves the right to commit any crime, to lie, to cheat" in order to attain their objectives.[2]

Alexander Haig and his successor as secretary of state, George P. Shultz, put a great deal of effort into forging a loose anti-Soviet alliance with Arabs and Israelis in the Middle East to thwart Soviet ambitions in that critical region. The administration instituted a massive buildup of the U.S. armed forces, both conventional and nuclear, with a view to deterring Soviet adventurism. In Central America, where leftists remained active throughout the 1980s, the Reagan administration took an exceptionally aggressive stance, announcing that it would not tolerate further Communist efforts to foment revolution there.

Central America quickly became an object of intense concern for the president and his advisory staff. One of the first actions of the new administration was to cut off economic aid to Nicaragua's Sandinista regime, which had assumed power in 1979, soon after Jimmy Carter had withdrawn U.S. support from its longtime ally Anastasio Somoza. Somoza was one of a long line of repressive leaders in Latin America who enjoyed the backing of the United States. Much like the Vietcong guerrillas in South Vietnam during the early 1960s, the

Sandinistas (named after Augusto César Sandino, a rebel leader who had fought against U.S. intervention in Nicaragua in the 1920s and early 1930s) gained a considerable following by promising to bring an end to human rights abuses, poverty, corruption, and Yankee imperialism.

The Reagan administration was skeptical in the extreme. The public utterances of the U.S. government focused on the Sandinistas' cozy relationship with the Soviet Union. Al Haig thought they were part of a wider Communist-led movement in the region, bent on establishing a Communist foothold in Latin America. Reagan's liberal critics saw them as progressive revolutionaries who were finally doing something about intractable poverty and repression. (Which picture was closer to the truth remains a subject of intense debate.)

In the waning days of the Carter administration, the Sandinista government demonstrated a growing distaste for free speech and political opposition parties. What's more, they were assembling a formidable army—the largest in the region—with the help of the Soviet Union.

The Reagan administration soon put the CIA covertly to work in an effort to destabilize the government of Nicaragua. The animosity of the United States toward the Sandinistas was fueled by their open support of Marxist guerrillas in the neighboring country of El Salvador. The American government had a considerable investment in that country; it had tried to encourage reforms and to diminish the numerous human rights abuses that afflicted El Salvador and, indeed, many other Latin American countries.

In January 1981 leftists in El Salvador launched the "Final Offensive" against the established government. The Sandinistas had provided the insurgents with moral support in addition to vast quantities of arms. The United States responded to the offensive, sending more than $10 million in arms and equipment to the government of El Salvador, as well as a limited number of military advisers.

An open election was held in March 1982 to determine who would govern in El Salvador. American officials supervised the election, but the results were not terribly encouraging for the United States. The leftists refused to participate, and a politician with links to death squads and other abuses, Roberto D'Aubuisson, was elected to the presidency rather than the U.S.-supported Christian Democratic candidate. The Reagan administration, by dangling the carrot of military and economic aid before D'Aubuisson, may have helped bring about some degree of democratic reform. The Salvadoran army made progress in the field against the leftist insurgency, but fighting continued between the government and the guerrillas until 1992, when a cease-fire was finally brokered.

The Reagan policy in Central America, governed as it was by the theme of anticommunism, had many critics. Conservatives thought Reagan was doing too little too late. Democrats in Congress, on the other hand, painted El Salvador as the next Vietnam—a small war on the verge of becoming bigger—and out of control. Ronald Steel, an associate at the Carnegie Endowment for International Peace, was among those who felt the administration was using political rhetoric to hide the true objective of U.S. policy: the maintenance of American control over the region. Steel wrote the following in an op-ed piece in 1983:

> Democracy is not why we are supporting the government of El Salvador, any more than why we were in Vietnam. If our "friends" win, the country will remain a despotism ruled by landlords through the army. If the guerrillas take over, it will probably also be a despotism ruled by the army and a cadre of ideologues. In either case, democracy is not the issue.[3]

The American people, for their part, were hardly enthusiastic about anything that had to do with Central America. They remained curiously unresponsive to the administration's claims that Communist activity in the region posed a serious threat to hemispheric security.

The president remained undaunted by either the lack of popular interest or criticism of his policies. The CIA, under the watchful eye of its director, William J. Casey, and National Security Council staff member Lieutenant Colonel Oliver North, trained and supplied a group of disgruntled Nicaraguan soldiers as guerrillas to challenge the Sandinistas. In March 1983 the Contras (as the CIA-trained guerrillas were called) left their secret bases in Honduras and crossed the border into Nicaragua to conduct guerrilla operations against the Sandinistas.

Their success was limited. President Reagan, anxious

to boost support for the Contra effort, began to refer to the Contras as freedom fighters. He even compared them to the Continental soldiers of the American Revolution, and he pressed Congress for more money to support their efforts. The Congress, led by Democrats who saw Reagan as a man bent on putting U.S. prestige at stake in a country of marginal significance, responded by passing the Boland Amendment, which placed a ban on appropriating funds for the "freedom fighters" for two years.

Frustrated by the failure of Congress to respond to what the administration said was a pressing matter of national security, Casey, North, and a number of other high-ranking officials and private citizens undertook to sell arms to Iran and illegally (in the opinion of most authorities) used the profits to fund the Contras. This eventually led to the greatest embarrassment of the Reagan administration, the Iran-Contra scandal, which greatly damaged the president's reputation and capacity to govern in the last several years of his tenure.

Other initiatives in the Reagan administration's first term were designed to challenge the Communists in the Western Hemisphere. The small West Indian island nation of Grenada in the Caribbean, only 133 square miles in area, had a leftist government with ties to the Soviet Union and Cuba. On the morning of October 25, 1983, U.S. Marines and Army Rangers landed on the island, which was defended by a small contingent of Cuban troops and armed Cuban construction workers. The Americans quickly dispatched these people and reestablished democratic rule.

The action was justified in part as a rescue mission.

Some eight hundred U.S. citizens, mostly medical students, were on the island, and in the anarchy that preceded the invasion their safety had been in question. In Grenada, there was proof that Reagan had not been imagining Communist plans to export revolution. A huge cache of weapons, enough for a ground force of some ten thousand men, was uncovered by U.S. troops.

The Grenada invasion raised uncomfortable questions. Many thoughtful people believed Reagan was doing a great deal more harm than good in undertaking such a mission, at least so far as long-term relations with Latin America were concerned. The United States' adventure incensed Latin Americans, who viewed what administration officials called a "rescue mission" as another example of blatant Yankee imperialism. Early in the twentieth century the United States had established political control over the entire region. Between 1900 and 1935, U.S. troops were sent, sometimes repeatedly, into Nicaragua, the Dominican Republic, Cuba, Mexico, Panama, and Haiti. Now, in Grenada, the colossus to the north appeared to be resuming that tradition.

Nevertheless, Grenada boosted American morale. It was one of those "splendid little wars" with a decisive finish. The administration hoped it would send a clear signal to Havana and Moscow that the United States was not going to sit by and let its neighbors slide into the Soviet camp.

The success in Grenada, however, was overshadowed by tragedy elsewhere. On October 23, 1983, 241 U.S. Marines had died in a terrorist bomb attack in Beirut, Lebanon. They were the victims of a suicidal Muslim truck driver who smashed through the marine lines and rammed into a high-rise building used as a barracks. (The Muslims had the impression that the U.S. "peace-keepers" were there to help Christian rivals with whom they were involved in a long and very violent struggle.) The marines had been in Beirut as part of a peacekeeping force following an Israeli invasion of Lebanon. The presence of U.S. troops was part of the Reagan administration's effort to establish a peace plan, to stabilize the region and keep out Soviet influence. But the peacekeepers were few in number and were prohibited from taking offensive action in the tinderbox that was Lebanon's capital city. The U.S. Marines were soon transformed from peacekeepers to targets and were quietly withdrawn in February 1984. The ancient hatreds and rivalries of the Middle East were more intractable and far less simple to solve than President Reagan had envisioned. Meanwhile, the fighting among many factions persisted in Lebanon.

Direct relations with the Soviets during Reagan's first term in office were marked by mistrust and by bitter outbursts from both sides. The Kremlin was surprised, even caught off guard, by the president's actions and pronouncements about the character of Russian leadership and about the Soviet Union's being an outlaw among nations. The Russians regarded the statements and Reagan's determination to build up U.S. military strength as deadly serious. Two weeks before his death in October 1982, Leonid Brezhnev* told his generals

*Brezhnev, the general secretary of the Communist Party, was succeeded by Yuri Andropov, formerly head of the KGB. Andropov died in February 1984 and was succeeded by Constantin Chernenko, who died less than a year later. Mikhail Gorbachev succeeded Chernenko.

that the Americans were pursuing a policy of "adventurism, rudeness and undisguised egoism" that "threatened to push the world into the flames of nuclear war."[4]

Relations between the superpowers were so grim in the early 1980s that newspapers and professional observers of U.S.–Soviet relations dubbed the period "Cold War II"—the second cold war, which had begun after the ending of détente. At the center of this era of heightened tension was the old issue of arms and arms control.

Reagan's strategy experts held that the Soviet Union would never negotiate seriously if it felt it was in a position of strength. If progress was to be made in arms control, reasoned Reagan and his advisers, the United States must rebuild its nuclear and conventional forces. The nation would then deal with the Soviets on arms control—and thus be more likely to secure arrangements favorable to the West. The administration expressed concern in public that the configuration of nuclear forces opened a "window of vulnerability"; in other words, the Russians might possibly be tempted to launch a devastating first strike that would leave the United States in a poor position to mount an adequate counterstrike.

Accordingly, Reagan pressed forward with a number of impressive, and expensive, new weapons systems, including a more deadly (and more difficult to detect) bomber, the B-1; a new class of submarine, the Trident II; and a multiple-warhead ICBM that would, the experts said, greatly reduce the temptation of Soviet planners to unleash the first nuclear strike against the United States.

The most grandiose and science-fiction-like new system was the Strategic Defense Initiative, or SDI. The president himself claimed credit for the idea behind SDI. Intended ultimately (that is, once the Russians had their own strategic defense system in place) to make offensive nuclear weapons obsolete, SDI called for the creation of a kind of protective dome over the United States. Defensive weapons, placed in space, would be programmed to knock out offensive missiles fired by the Soviets.

Although most scientists found SDI impracticable, the Reagan administration thought it could lead to the end of the costly arms race between the superpowers. Once the Americans and the Soviets had their systems in place, offensive weapons would be rendered obsolete. Critics, of whom there were many, scoffed at this notion, claiming that the Soviets would be more likely to interpret the new initiative as a destabilizer—or even more ominously, as a first step on the way to an actual strike aimed at the Soviet Union. If the United States were effectively shielded from Soviet missiles, the Soviets could hardly mount a strike. The critics appeared to be correct. We now know that SDI worried the Soviets a great deal. The Kremlin unsuccessfully offered a number of proposals to entice the United States into giving up the program altogether.

Another U.S. initiative that worried the Kremlin was the October 1983 deployment of a new class of American-built cruise missiles in Britain and West Germany. The missiles numbered some five hundred and were designed to counter the threat posed by the

Soviet SS-20 intermediate-range nuclear missiles recently installed in Eastern Europe. The SS-20s were aimed at the military bases and population centers of Western Europe, not at the United States, and their presence had shaken NATO considerably. When the United States acted to counter the Soviet deployment, the Russians walked out of arms control negotiations, which had been proceeding (with no success to speak of) for several years.

Late 1983 was a sobering time for East-West relations. Although proposals for arms reductions were proffered by both sides, it often seemed that these were put forward with a view to securing a propaganda victory. Many questioned whether there was a sincere desire on the part of either party to control the buildup. In fact, as the charts on pages 222–23 show, nuclear weapons were deployed at a disturbing rate throughout the 1980s.

Meanwhile, the actions of the Soviets served to confirm the U.S. president's dark view of the Soviet Union as unwilling to accept the unwritten rules of civilized behavior. When Solidarity, a reform-minded trade union of great power and popularity, emerged as a political force in Poland in 1980 and 1981, the Soviets moved to crush it by installing a hard-line Communist, General Wojciech Jaruzelski, as premier. Jaruzelski quickly imposed martial law and imprisoned hundreds of Solidarity officials, including Lech Walesa, the movement's leader. Ronald Reagan expressed outrage, but he could do little to curb Soviet behavior. To the outside world, and to the Poles themselves, the Kremlin's actions in Poland demonstrated the rigidity and ruthlessness of the Soviet political system.

Then in September 1983, the world was shocked by a Soviet action of unprecedented brutality and callousness. Soviet jets shot down a South Korean airliner that appeared to have strayed into Soviet airspace, killing 269 people. For a week the Kremlin refused to admit it knew anything about the tragedy. When it finally confessed that Soviet jets had been involved, no apology of any kind was offered to either the South Korean government or the victims' families.

By the time Reagan's first term was coming to a close, the United States was recovering from the trauma of Vietnam and was once again ready and willing to use force in the international arena. The United States was no longer the "helpless giant" (as Richard Nixon had once termed it) of the 1970s, unsure of itself and of the role of force in international affairs. In the Caribbean, in the Middle East, in Central America, wherever Reagan and his foreign-policy advisers had sensed Communist probing or, for that matter, other potential threats to U.S. interests, the president had proved willing—many felt too willing—to stand up to the challenge. He vigorously supported SDI and the buildup of conventional and nuclear forces, consistently defending those expensive programs as essential elements in the quest to establish a safer, more secure, and more democratic inter-national environment.

Critics portrayed the Reagan foreign-policy team as "shoot from the hip" types—conservative ideologues whose ideas were more appropriate to the 1950s, when the United States had enjoyed a wide margin of strategic superiority over its great rival. The time was long

THE ARMS RACE: GROWTH OF U.S. AND USSR NUCLEAR WEAPONS ARSENALS, 1946–91

YEAR	NATION	ICBMs[1]	SLBMs[2]	BOMBERS	TOTALS
1946	U.S.	—	—	125	125
	USSR	—	—	—	—
1950	U.S.	—	—	462	462
	USSR	—	—	—	—
1956	U.S.	—	—	1,470	1,470
	USSR	—	—	22	22
1960	U.S.	12	32	1,515	1,559
	USSR	4	30	104	138
1965	U.S.	854	384	650	1,888
	USSR	225	75	163	463
1970	U.S.	1,054	656	390	2,100
	USSR	1,361	317	157	1,835
1975	U.S.	1,054	656	396	2,106
	USSR	1,587	771	157	2,515
1980	U.S.	1,054	592	376	2,022
	USSR	1,398	990	157	2,545
1985	U.S.	1,020	648	297	1,965
	USSR	1,398	980	160	2,538
1987	U.S.	1,000	640	361	2,001
	USSR	1,418	962	165	2,545
1988	U.S.	1,000	640	337	1,977
	USSR	1,346	978	175	2,499
1989	U.S.	1,000	608	372	1,980
	USSR	1,451	960	195	2,606
1990	U.S.	1,000	624	277	1,901
	USSR	1,398	930	175	2,503
1991	U.S.	1,000	640	277	1,917
	USSR	1,388	912	177	2,477

1. Intercontinental ballistic missiles 2. Submarine launched ballistic missiles Note: These figures are for launchers—the rockets or aircraft carrying the nuclear weapons. After 1970, the number of warheads, or specific weapons, grew larger than the number of launchers (refer to the following chart). This was a result of the introduction of multiple warheads (MRVS and MIRVS) so that one missile could carry several warheads, each capable of being aimed at a different target. Source: Natural Resources Defense Council, *Nuclear Weapons Databook* (1994).

The Arms Race: Total U.S. and USSR Nuclear Warheads 1946–91

YEAR	U.S.	USSR
1946	9	0
1950	400	0
1956	2,123	84
1960	3,117	354
1965	4,251	829
1970	4,960	2,216
1975	9,828	3,217
1980	10,608	7,480
1985	11,974	10,012
1987	13,002	10,442
1988	13,012	11,546
1989	13,000	11,662
1990	12,102	11,420
1991	11,966	10,980

Note: These figures are for strategic nuclear warheads only. Source: Natural Resources Defense Council and *SIPRI Yearbook: World Armaments and Disarmament.* Oxford University Press, 1988–91.

past, it was often argued, for the use of force to achieve diplomatic ends. It had no place in a world with a staggering quantity of nuclear weaponry. It was pointed out, too, that the Reagan team was foolishly assuming that all of the world's considerably complex and varied problems were caused by the machinations of the Communists. Reagan, for his part, dismissed the critics as naysayers and cynics who had forgotten that force and power in the hands of the righteous could be used to orchestrate change for the good.

Beginning in 1984, critics as well as supporters of the

former California governor began to detect a change in his attitude and, more generally, in the U.S.–Soviet relationship. A new Soviet leader came to the fore in February 1984; the State Department knew very little about Konstantin Chernenko. Many speculated that he would at least try to soften the hard edges of the super-power relationship. November 1984 was an election year in the United States, and the president showed a genuine desire to tone down his anti-Soviet rhetoric. Perhaps it was true, as some newspaper columnists said, that Reagan wanted to go down in history not as the hardest in a long line of hard-line anti-Communists, but as a statesman who cemented a better relationship with the Soviet Union so the world might become a safer place.

In any event, in 1984 the White House's public statements concerning the Soviet Union were undeniably more conciliatory and certainly less strident than in earlier years. One barometer of change came in the fall of 1984, when veteran Soviet Foreign Minister Andrey Gromyko appeared in Washington for a chat with Ronald Reagan. The very presence of this diplomat in the bosom of official Washington came as something of a shock, given all the hostile feelings of the preceding four years.

As it turned out, the meeting marked the beginning of a new and more constructive period in U.S.–Soviet relations. The great change in the texture of super-power interaction was in part brought about by surprising events in Eastern Europe and the Soviet Union: the reunification of Germany, the collapse of Soviet control over Eastern Europe, and finally in December 1991, the passing away of the Soviet Union itself. At the same time, it seems doubtful that those internal developments would have unfolded as they did had not two individuals, Ronald Reagan and Mikhail Gorbachev, forged a constructive personal relationship.

All of these happy developments were a long way off as 1985 approached. The most significant event of that year concerning the cold war was the emergence of Mikhail Gorbachev, a trained economist, as the pre-eminent political figure in the USSR. Gorbachev was the first Soviet leader who recognized that the Soviet Communist Party and the apparatus it had set up to govern the Soviet Union were deeply flawed and incapable of continuing a highly expensive arms race with the United States.

Gorbachev was hardly cut from the same cloth as most senior Soviet officials of the Brezhnev era. He'd been a loyal ally of Andropov, who'd had the misfortune to die before he had accomplished much. But Gorbachev was a risk taker, a bold and audacious politi-cian who refused to think or act in old established pat-terns. The first Soviet leader to be born after the Russian Revolution, he commanded a great deal of respect among younger members of the Party, in large measure because he had demonstrated a willingness to make dif-ficult decisions and to implement change, even if it made him enemies.

Elected to the post of general secretary by the Central Committee of the Communist Party of the Soviet Union, Gorbachev stunned the conservatives with a series of initiatives designed to break down the Party's monopoly of power. The tight grip of the Communist Party on Soviet life and thought began to give way. For the first time the people were able to air their true concerns, and the magnitude of the system's failure became public.

The people of the Soviet Union did not have enough to eat. The economy was falling behind those of the Western countries. In 1970 the Soviet gross national product, the sum total of all the goods its people had produced, was growing at a rate of about five percent a year. By 1979, the figure had dropped to one percent. More ominously, the infant mortality rate had moved in the wrong direction.

On the international front, the weapons race with the United States had led to neglect of consumer industries, which in turn had triggered unrest and deep dissatisfaction with the Party. Surveying the social and political landscape of his troubled country, Gorbachev came to the conclusion that he faced, as one observer put it, "a deepening crisis in almost every aspect of Soviet life, including foreign policy."[5]

And so Gorbachev acted. His new policies, designed to curb the downward spiral, were called *glasnost,* meaning "openness," and *perestroika,* which roughly translates as "restructuring." What most desperately needed restructuring was the Soviet economic system. The centrally planned economy, with its thousands of bureaucrats, was highly inefficient and rotten with corruption. Goods, whether perishables such as meat or durables such as cars or washing machines, were of inferior quality to those produced by the free-market economies of the West. Gorbachev ordered many changes, including the introduction of free markets and profit incentives, hoping to increase efficiency and thus expand the total output of the Soviet economy.

Glasnost was applied, beginning in the mid-1980s, to all aspects of Soviet life. In homes, in government, in schools, glasnost called for a new honesty, a willingness to admit that the rigid socialist order had not always been effective in meeting the challenges of modern life and that mistakes had been made by the government and the Party. Gorbachev relaxed censorship of the written and spoken word.

Soon professors, writers, artists, and ordinary citizens throughout the Soviet Union were openly talking about the failures of their economic system, about the corruption in the factories, about the lies concerning twentieth-century history the Communists had fed to Soviet citizens for decades. Searching articles were written and published that questioned the performance of the socialist model as devised by past Soviet leaders. Sometimes there was a wistful tone to the analyses. Some were tinged with pessimism:

> Imperialist ideologues are rushing to interpret what is happening as a historic defeat for socialism. . . . Was the model of socialism we built the only possible one . . . ? Under the form of socialism that took shape . . . socialism's principal economic task—overtaking capitalism in labor productivity and per capita output—was not solved. . . . Apathy and social passivity grew . . . ;

the management system . . . had completely exhausted its capabilities. Retaining it was causing economic stagnation, bringing our society to the brink of a crisis, and weakening the Soviet Union's prestige and influence in the international arena.[6]

The great figures of Soviet communism, Stalin and Lenin, men who were revered, for the first time were examined in light of their true actions, not what the Communist Party-produced textbooks and newspapers and documentaries had *said* were their actions.

Even the basic philosophical tenets of communism were brought into serious question. In his book *Perestroika*, Gorbachev greatly softened the party line on one of communism's grand themes, class struggle, thus signaling the West that he was sincerely looking for a new, less hostile relationship. "Ideological differences," wrote the general secretary, "should not be transferred to the sphere of interstate relations nor should foreign policy be subordinate to them, for ideologies [that is, those of communism and democracy] may be poles apart, whereas the interests of survival and prevention of war stand universal and supreme."[7] To put it in plain language, communism's triumph was no longer as important as survival and prevention of nuclear war. It was an astonishing and welcome statement.

Without these great and painful changes in the Soviet leadership, the process of ending the cold war could not have begun. But it takes two to dance, and in the person of Ronald Reagan, Gorbachev found, to the surprise of many people, a willing partner.

Soon after Gorbachev assumed the leadership of his country, he received a letter from President Reagan, inviting him to a summit in Washington. Gorbachev was receptive; under the circumstances in which he found himself, there could be much to be gained in a face-to-face meeting with the U.S. president. Gorbachev's response to the letter was hopeful. He said he was interested in establishing a relationship of peaceful competition, not confrontation, with the United States. It took well over half a year to square away the details of the meeting. It was decided that the two would meet at the neutral site of Geneva, Switzerland; they did so in November 1985.

The discussions at this first summit focused on the issue of nuclear weapons. The talks were frank and direct. Gorbachev insisted that reductions in the Soviet nuclear arsenal were inconceivable while SDI development continued. Reagan, however, was determined not to abandon his pet defense project, and the conference ended with only one agreement: The two would meet again and try to work out an arms reduction treaty.

At the second summit, this one in the unlikely setting of Reykjavík Iceland, Gorbachev called for a unilateral halt to nuclear testing, among other initiatives. He had done what no previous Soviet leader had been able to do: earn a reputation as a world-class statesman with a sincere interest in peace. Reagan, meanwhile, realized that the U.S. federal debt was larger than it had ever been in American history and also that he was now bargaining from a position of strength. It would be a good time to reach an accommodation.

At Reykjavík, the two negotiating teams talked optimistically about a number of arrangements, including the dismantling of all nuclear weapons within ten years. Here, too, however, hopes were dashed in the end. The two teams produced a workable agreement on offensive weapons cuts, but once again SDI proved to be a stumbling block. The Russians would not put their signature on anything until the president had agreed to limit SDI research. The agreement on offensive weapons had to be trashed.

Nevertheless, observers in Iceland did detect one positive development. Reagan and Gorbachev were clearly establishing a warm and trusting (by superpower standards) personal relationship. They genuinely seemed to like each other. Gorbachev found many of Reagan's jokes and stories amusing, and he would even offer a few jokes of his own, often on the subject of Soviet bureaucracy. The warmth of their relationship, coupled with the growing pressure of world opinion to reduce tensions, encouraged their respective experts to find a way around the considerable strategic differences and complexities that always attended negotiations on weapons of mass destruction.

At the third summit, in December 1987 in Washington, there was measurable progress on the arms control front. On December 8, the two men sat at a table once used by President Abraham Lincoln and signed an agreement that had taken many months and thousands of hours of labor to produce. It would lead, over the course of three years, to the destruction of 859 U.S. missiles and more than 1,800 Soviet missiles with ranges from 300 to 3,400 miles, all of them situated in Europe.

The INF (Intermediate-Range Nuclear Forces) Treaty was an important document in cold war history. For the first time, the adversaries agreed not only to destroy nuclear weapons but also to give the opposite party the capacity to verify by on-site inspection that such destruction had taken place.

Another remarkable development of the Washington summit was that Gorbachev had captured the imagination of Americans everywhere. Despite his position as head of state of the USSR, many people in the United States trusted this man. He was cheered enthusiastically, especially when his motorcade made several unplanned stops in Washington so he could walk among the crowds and shake hands—a very American political gesture. The Soviet leader's popularity continued to grow in the United States after he announced in February 1988 that he would begin to withdraw Soviet troops from Afghanistan.

Ronald Reagan was not doing too badly in the eyes of the Soviet people, either. When he went to Moscow in the spring of 1988 for a fourth and final meeting with Gorbachev, he was received by enthusiastic crowds.

By the time the great "Red hater," Ronald Reagan, found himself in Moscow, the end of the cold war was already in sight. Throughout 1988 and 1989, the pace of change accelerated. Relations between the superpowers had vastly improved by this point, and during these two years the dominant news stories regarding international affairs did not concern the superpowers so much as events within the Eastern bloc. Americans, including their new president, Republican George Bush, were primarily onlookers.

In the Soviet Union, Gorbachev and other progressives (notably Boris Yeltsin) struggled against reactionaries and conservatives to break down the repressive system of government, to reintroduce open debate and discussion after a seventy-year absence, and to privatize and decentralize the economy. The drive for reform in the Soviet Union couldn't be contained within the borders of that country; other reform movements rapidly gained momentum in the Communist-controlled nations of Eastern Europe. Soon the impossible seemed to be happening: The Eastern Europeans were openly pursuing complete independence from the Soviets, and to the astonishment of the world, the Soviets did not send in the troops.

The process of breaking down old institutions and designing new ones was tricky, fraught with pitfalls. One of the key steps in the disintegration of Communist Party power in the Soviet Union occurred on December 1, 1988, when the USSR's nominal parliament, the Supreme Soviet, voted to approve radical changes in the political structure of the country. The fifteen-hundred-member body, which had in effect rubber-stamped the orders of the Politburo, was to be made into a two-house legislature in 1989. Most of its members would be elected at the local level by ordinary Soviet citizens. It was an astonishing development. In a speech to legislators before the vote, Gorbachev, sounding more like James Madison than a Soviet politician, said the revisions were necessary to "exclude the possibility of the state machinery getting beyond the control of the people and their representatives."[8]

In March 1989, the first election in which more than one candidate was allowed to run took place in the Soviet Union. The election brought in the first Soviet elected body that might be said to be democratic. Many of those elected criticized the Communist Party openly and called for its demise. Meanwhile, the Baltic republics—Latvia, Estonia, and Lithuania—declared their independence from Moscow. No Soviet tanks rolled forward. There were similar, if less intense, stirrings in all the other Soviet-controlled republics.

It was somehow fitting that the first non-Communist government in Eastern Europe should emerge in Poland, where the most recent quest for self-determination had begun in 1981, with Lech Walesa's Solidarity trade union. In April 1989, after complicated negotiations, an agreement was reached between reformers and Communists on the restructuring of Polish political institutions. In August of that year, journalist and Solidarity member Tadeuz Mazowiecki became premier of Poland.

It was later revealed that the Polish Communist Party leader had called Gorbachev for advice and support because it was becoming clear that his party was about to lose power. To Mazowiecki's immense surprise, Gorbachev told him to join with the reformers. There would be no Soviet intervention to save the day for the Polish Communists. An important and uplifting signal had been sent to reform-minded peoples throughout the region.

Everywhere else in Eastern Europe, at greater and lesser speeds, people were actively dismantling the institutions of Communist dominance and replacing them with democratic ones. Hungary, in May 1989, dispensed with its Communist Party altogether and tore down the 150-mile-long fence along its border with neutral Austria, thus allowing (albeit, indirectly) the East Germans free movement to the West. A door had opened in the Iron Curtain.

In the summer of 1989, hundreds, and then thousands, of East Germans crossed the border into Hungary. Most were on a journey that would take them through that country to Austria, and then on to relatives, friends, and a more prosperous life in West Germany. East Germany as a country began to crumble away, its authority vanishing before the power of mass demonstrations for freedom in Liepzig, Berlin, and Dresden. Erich Honecker, the longtime general secretary of the East German Communist Party, tried desperately to hold on to power; but the legitimacy of his regime completely collapsed. Honecker, as broken and demoralized as the government he had long ruled, eventually fled the country.

Reform had turned to revolution. On November 9, 1989, the greatest symbol of the cold war—the Berlin Wall—came down. There was no shooting, no combat of any kind. The East German government announced that its people could now leave through any crossing point they could find. They did, as television cameras from all over the world recorded the astounding event, the likes of which no one, even a year earlier, had dreamed possible.

The sight of ordinary Germans, from both East and West, taking up picks and shovels against the Berlin Wall (huge hunks of which were broken down and sold throughout the world, notably in the United States) swept away the lingering doubts of even the most hardened skeptics that the long cold war was coming to an end.

The rivalry between communism and democracy, now forty-five years old, hadn't long to live. The conflict began in Germany, its earliest crises had unfolded there, and there, it appeared, the cold war would end. Later that November, the nations of the Warsaw Pact jointly condemned the Brezhnev Doctrine, the statement of policy that had justified Soviet intervention in Eastern Europe. The joint statement labeled the policy illegal. In the future, no state that had been a member of the pact would interfere in another former member's internal affairs.

The events of 1989, explosive though they were, foreshadowed even greater changes. In 1990 and 1991, the Soviet president who had made the transformation of Eastern Europe possible tried to use his considerable status and skill to keep his own nation from splintering. But the old forces and ideas of ethnic self-determination and independence had a deep hold on people throughout the Soviet Union, and their resentments of the institutions of the Soviet state proved too great.

In February of 1990, the Communist Party of the Soviet Union officially renounced its monopoly on political power. The reformers had won a major victory. Then in September, the USSR relinquished all its claims on the territory that had been East Germany. No one had expected Moscow, with its obsession for security, to do that. On the first day of October came another breakthrough: the Supreme Soviet passed legislation guaranteeing religious freedom to all citizens.

Meanwhile, diplomats worked to define and formalize new attitudes and circumstances in international politics. In November 1990, eleven presidents (including George Bush and Mikhail Gorbachev), twenty-two premiers, and many foreign ministers gathered in Paris for the Conference on Security and Cooperation in Europe. The discussions were frank and upbeat. At the conclusion of the meeting, the leaders signed the Treaty on Conventional Armed Forces in Europe, which placed strict limits on the number of tanks, artillery, and aircraft that any nation could amass on that continent. President Bush hailed the pact as "the most far-reaching arms agreement" ever negotiated.[9] President Gorbachev, elated by all that had transpired, exclaimed, "What a long way the world has come!"[10]

As the diplomats worked, the situation in the USSR grew more volatile. Chaos threatened to break out, as the peoples of the various Soviet republics* rose up against the central government and demanded independence. The year 1991 was one of ceaseless turmoil and endless negotiation and squabbling among the

---

*Throughout the period covered in this book, the Soviet Union consisted of fifteen different administrative or governmental entities called republics. They all differed in size and ethnic makeup, and governments of the individual republics had little real governing power when compared to that of the Politburo in Moscow.

many political parties and factions that surfaced across the Soviet Union.

In August 1991, a coup against Gorbachev by the hard-liners threatened the democracy movement, but the people rose up against those who hoped to restore the old repressive order and a new hero of the revolution emerged: Boris Yeltsin. Gorbachev was, in effect, forced to resign, a victim of the very forces he had worked so hard to unleash.

Unlike Gorbachev, Yeltsin had no interest in preserving the Soviet Union as a political entity. The energies and efforts of the reformers, he felt, would best be put to use in creating a new form of government, unhindered by connection with the institutions of an old and corrupt regime. On December 19, 1991, Yeltsin issued a decree directing the government of the Republic of Russia to take over the Kremlin, for seventy years the seat of power for the Soviet Union.

Then, on December 21, representatives of all eleven remaining republics of the USSR signed agreements creating a new, rather loosely defined Commonwealth of Independent States (CIS). On December 25, 1991, about a half hour after Mikhail Gorbachev formally resigned as the last general secretary of the Communist Party, the red hammer-and-sickle flag of the Union of Soviet Socialist Republics was lowered, replaced atop the Kremlin by the white, red, and blue flag of czarist pre-revolutionary Russia. The Soviet Union, America's great superpower rival and cold war nemesis, ceased to exist.

CHAPTER ELEVEN

REFLECTIONS

The resurgence of democracy and the end of repression in Eastern Europe and among the peoples of the Soviet Union were remarkable and happy events in a century cursed with more killing and horror than any other in recorded history. That the cold war had ended in victory for the United States, for democratic values over those espoused by communism, seemed obvious to most observers. But what explained the victory? How successful was the American crusade against communism, and what were the consequences of the cold war? Finally, what might happen now that the era of the great superpower rivalry is over?

Explanations of the outcome varied. Supporters of Presidents Reagan and Bush, who had orchestrated the immense buildup and modernization of U.S. military forces in the 1980s, gave these two American leaders and their tough-talking predecessors a good deal of the credit. They pointed out that the Reagan-Bush strategy had been right from the start: A vigorous defense establishment and an active effort to counter Soviet moves in the 1980s had forced the Soviets to retreat, licking their wounds, from their international adventurism. Recognizing that communism was foundering in the world at large and in the Soviet Union in particular, Gorbachev tried to save his nation by removing all of its ideological underpinnings.

Bush and Reagan were, of course, hardly strategic pathfinders in this regard, for their policy was in many ways a continuation of containment, the doctrine that all U.S. presidents had followed since the days of Harry Truman. So it was that George Kennan, the father of containment, appeared to be something of a prophet. As long ago as 1947, Kennan had stated that the constant pressures applied by the West against the expansive impulses of the Kremlin would in time lead to the break-up of Soviet power.

But long-term U.S. policy alone doesn't explain the collapse of communism in the Eastern bloc. Much of the credit for the withering away of Communist governments rests with the peoples of the Soviet Union and its satellite nations—they waged a spiritual struggle against the lies, corruptions, and oppressions that were the stock in trade of their governments for decades. Then, of course, there was the Communist system itself. For the human beings who lived under it, the system simply did not provide a satisfactory way of life. Nor did communism demonstrate any real capacity to address social and economic problems as they arose—something at which the capitalist democracies proved to be surprisingly adept. In this sense, the legacy of the Bolshevik Revolution collapsed under its own weight.

For the Soviet Union, far more than any other country, the waging of the cold war had exacted a devastating toll. The USSR, whose economic output from 1945 to 1991 was far smaller than that of the United States, maintained its superpower status largely by ignoring the needs and general welfare of its people. The maintenance and support of the mighty Red Army, and the development of a nuclear arsenal to equal that of the United States were the top priorities of the Soviet leadership. Throughout the cold war, the Soviets spent a far greater proportion of their resources on defense spending than the Americans did. Over many years the Soviets had spent about fifteen percent of their gross national product (that is, their total output of goods and services) on defense, not civilian needs. In the end, it was the nearly total disregard for its people that crushed the Soviet government and the ideas upon which it was based.

How successful were the United States policies described in this book? Because only a handful of years have passed since the end of the cold war, any answer to this question must be provisional. The answer also depends on one's definition of "success." It is true that when the crusade against communism ended there were far more people who could shape their own destiny and reap the benefits of the collective security system that U.S. leaders had envisioned at the end of World War II. That had been a major objective of United States foreign policy, and it was at the core of the nation's anti-Communist crusade.

In geopolitical terms, containment had worked well. Soviet expansionism was successfully checked in Europe, and thanks to the dedication and restraint of leadership in both the United States and the Soviet Union, outright war between the world's great powers was avoided for more than forty years. This was an enormous achievement when one considers the regularity of major conflict in world affairs over the last five hundred years.

The results of containment and the anticommunist crusade beyond Europe were far more ambiguous, particularly in Asia and Central America. It is one of the many ironies of the cold war that the moral revulsion U.S. policy makers felt for communism obscured clear and pragmatic thinking about those peoples and regions and about how the United States could best aid the rise of truly democratic institutions. Time and again, the United States evaluated political leaders around the world not in terms of their abilities and their objectives but in terms of their level of hostility to communism. Even when Communist leaders demonstrated their independence from Moscow (Ho Chi Minh in Vietnam and Mao in China are prime examples), the United States would have little or nothing to do with them. So it was that America lost countless opportunities to effect democratic reform in places such as Yugoslavia, Vietnam, Nicaragua, and China.

As historian John Lewis Gaddis observed,

For decades after the onset of the Cold War, the United States officially took the view that adherence to Marxism-Leninism not only made governments internally repressive but also—through their presumed subservience to Moscow—a threat to the global balance of power. There was never very good evidence to support these claims. . . . The inability to understand that in certain parts of the world one could be a communist and a nationalist at the same time contributed to [among other problems] a . . . disastrous American involvement in Indochina.[1]

What is more, the obsession with communism often blinded the United States to the realities and problems faced by other countries. Communist activity in Asia and Latin America was a result of poverty, exploitation, and loss of hope, not (as the various U.S. administrations had argued) its cause. Because of this one-dimensional thinking (and policy making), the United States came to be seen by many peoples as a kind of oafish giant, obsessed with the evil machinations of world communism.

And what of the anticommunist crusade's effects on the United States? Chapter five describes how potent a force anticommunism became, how it altered the landscape of politics and culture. Anticommunist ideas and themes permeated the consciousness of all Americans in the cold war era.

But the effects of the American crusade went beyond that. As he was about to leave office in January 1961, Dwight David Eisenhower reminded Americans that the basic objective of U.S. national security policy was "maintaining the security of the United States and the vitality of its fundamental values and institutions." Ike knew that a healthy economy was one of those institutions; he worried that the "military-industrial complex," the constellation of the armed services and the defense industries that relied on the cold war for their livelihood, would drive the country into debt, destroying the great vitality of the U.S. economy. Who can deny that such a "complex" exists, and that in large measure it was one of the unwanted consequences of waging the cold war? Many Americans who lived through the 1980s remember the almost constant reports of enormous waste and fraud in the Pentagon's various weapons procurement programs and of the intensive lobbying efforts of the defense industries and their supporters in Washington.

What Ike feared would happen has happened, to some extent. Between 1945 and 1991, the United States spent roughly seven percent of its gross national product on defense. The huge defense expenditures had not been completely paid for with taxes. The government had been forced to borrow money—and a great deal of it. When Ronald Reagan left office, the total federal debt stood at a staggering $2.6 trillion (see the table in the appendix for more information on defense spending and federal debt).

The government spending that went along with that debt had created jobs and prosperity in the 1980s. But in the 1990s, more and more economists worried about the consequences of the growing federal deficit. The debt (the total amount the U.S. government owed to private institutions and investors, many of whom were foreign) would have to be worked off by future generations of Americans. For in the final analysis, governments obtain all their funds from taxes levied on their citizens. If the economists are correct, then the cold war will have played no small role in deflating a long-cherished American myth—that each generation will enjoy a higher standard of living than the previous one.

Other myths fell by the wayside as a result of the long conflict with communism. Most Americans had believed that the United States conducted its foreign policy in a manner consonant with its moral and political ideals. U.S. decision makers, however, whether by design or necessity (the answer depends very much on one's politics), were given to lying, deceiving, and putting into effect any number of morally questionable policies and activities. The extensive use of covert operations and CIA funds to attempt to overthrow unfriendly regimes in Iran, Guatemala, and Cuba are just three examples from a lengthy list.

Then, of course, there was the government's disinformation campaign concerning the war in Vietnam, and there was the Watergate scandal, which resulted ultimately from President Nixon's desire to run that war without interference from others in or outside of government. In addition, many felt that the government was covering up its own irresponsible behavior regarding nuclear waste. There is evidence that improper disposal of nuclear waste is leading to premature death and disease among the people who live near nuclear weapons testing sites.

Americans in the 1990s are no longer willing to believe much of what their government tells them, and the effort to break down the walls of government secrecy in foreign affairs has been going on in earnest since the 1960s. To cite one example, a movement has been under way since 1993 to expose how the CIA and other intelligence agencies spent (and continue to spend) their secret "black budget"—the $20 to $30 billion those agencies have at their disposal for which they provide no accounting.

Cold war policies have been at least partially responsible for the erosion of faith between the American people and their government. The government usually justified those policies as necessary evils in a life-and-death struggle against people (and an ideology) bent on destroying the democratic way of life. Were they justified? There is no one, correct answer to that question.

For the United States, the fight against communism amounted to nothing less than a defining national mission. With the collapse of communism in Eastern Europe and the Soviet Union a matter of history, what was the next great challenge? the next key objective in world affairs? The end of the rivalry with the Soviets sent men and women in the foreign-policy think tanks, as well as people in government, into a protracted period of soul-searching and rethinking. Just what were the goals of the United States in the 1990s? What was the new definition of the national interest? Where were the new threats?

One thing was clear, however. Great changes would take shape in the world of international affairs. For the first time in forty-five years, no military power posed a threat to the territorial integrity of Europe. No great-power rivalry existed anywhere in the world. Nor did any nation have the capacity to seriously threaten the United States with military force.

These developments led many analysts in the early 1990s to speak hearteningly of a "peace dividend" for the United States. Defense budgets could be cut and more money spent on solutions to the pressing domestic problems confronting the country, from homelessness, poverty, hunger, inadequate health care, and strife-filled race relations to unemployment and a crumbling transportation infrastructure. Those who hoped for such a windfall, however, may have misjudged what lay ahead.

A host of intractable problems surfaced. Among the most prominent of these are the tragic ethnic conflicts in what had been Yugoslavia and in the African nation of Rwanda. Ominous signs are on the horizon in the former republics of the USSR, especially in Russia, where hard-liners have recently made gains over those who seek progressive reform. In the heart of Europe, extremist groups spouting ideas similar to those of Nazi Germany's leaders are gaining strength. The proliferation of nuclear powers is a great worry and one with which the international community will have to cope over the coming decade.

Indeed, since the demise of the Soviet Union, the general level of chaos on the international scene seems to have increased. Self-determination has brought many headaches. "From Haiti in the Western Hemisphere to the remnants of Yugoslavia," wrote Gerald B. Helman and Steven R. Ratner in the magazine *Foreign Affairs,* "from Somalia, Sudan and Liberia in Africa to Cambodia in Southeast Asia, a disturbing new phenomenon is emerging: the failed nation state, utterly incapable of sustaining itself as a member of the international community."[2]

It may very well be that the United Nations, which in recent years has assumed a more authoritative role in dealing with wars and other crises, will be calling upon the unique capabilities of American power and diplomacy to help manage trouble around the world. If this happens and if the Americans are prepared to overcome the long-standing isolationist impulse that has once again emerged (this time in the absence of a Soviet threat), the United States may be able to make a significant contribution to the betterment of the world.

Will the United States, with all its problems and woes, be up to the task? The answer depends largely on the energies, inclinations, and ideas of young Americans, men and women who have lived through part of a cold war waged by older generations.

SELECTED CHRONOLOGY OF THE COLD WAR 1945–91

1945

April 12: Franklin Delano Roosevelt dies. Harry S Truman assumes presidency of the United States.

May 8: World War II in Europe ends.

July–August: Churchill, Stalin, and Truman meet at Potsdam, Germany, to discuss the shape of postwar Europe.

August 6: The United States drops the first atomic bomb used in war on Hiroshima, Japan.

August 14: Japan accepts terms for surrendering unconditionally to the Allies.

1946

February 22: George F. Kennan sends his "Long Telegram" to Washington, outlining the policy of containment.

March 5: In a speech at Westminster College in Fulton,

Missouri, Winston Churchill warns of an Iron Curtain being drawn across Europe.

1947

March 12: In a speech before Congress, Truman outlines the doctrine that bears his name.

June 5: Secretary of State George C. Marshall proposes the Marshall Plan at the Harvard University commencement.

July 25: Truman signs the National Security Act, establishing a unified Department of Defense and creating the National Security Council.

October 18: The House Un-American Activities Committee opens an investigation of Communist infiltration in the movie industry.

December 19: Congress votes a $540 million appropriation for interim aid to France, Italy, Austria, and China, and receives Truman's request for $17 billion for a four-year economic recovery program for Europe.

1948

February: Soviet-backed coup in Czechoslovakia puts a Communist regime in power, creating a war scare in the United States and the Soviet Union.

March 6: The United States and its Western European allies reach agreement on the formation of a government for West Germany.

April 2: Congress approves the Marshall Plan.

June 24: Soviet occupation forces begin a blockade of Berlin.

August 3: Former Communist Whittaker Chambers

names Alger Hiss as a former Communist before the House Un-American Activities Committee.

November 2: Truman defeats Republican Thomas Dewey in the presidential election.

1949

April 4: Twelve nations, including the United States, sign the North Atlantic Treaty, thereby bringing the North Atlantic Treaty Organization (NATO) into existence.

May 12: Soviet blockade of Berlin ends.

September 23: Truman announces that the Soviet Union has exploded an atomic bomb.

October 1: A Communist regime under Mao Zedong is established in China.

1950

January 21: Alger Hiss is convicted of perjury.

February 9: In Wheeling, West Virginia, Senator Joseph R. McCarthy claims to know of 205 Communists in the U.S. State Department.

June 25: North Korea invades South Korea.

June 30: Truman orders U.S. ground forces into Korea and extends the draft to July 1951.

October 26: The Chinese enter the Korean War and fight the NATO forces.

1951

April 11: Truman relieves General Douglas MacArthur of his command in Korea, replacing him with General Matthew B. Ridgway.

July 7: Ridgway, as commander of UN forces in Korea, begins cease-fire negotiations with China and North Korea.

1952

May 1: The U.S. State Department bans travel to the Soviet Union and its satellites.

November 1: The United States tests the first hydrogen bomb.

1953

January 20: Dwight David Eisenhower is sworn in as thirty-fourth president of the United States.

March 5: Marshal Joseph Stalin of the Soviet Union dies.

June 17: Riots break out in East Germany over shortages and increased work quotas. Soviet tanks move in to quell the demonstrations.

July 27: The United States and North Korea sign an armistice in Panmunjom, thus ending the Korean War.

August 12: The Soviet Union explodes its first hydrogen bomb.

August 19–22: A CIA-sponsored coup in Iran results in the installation of a pro-Western government.

1954

January 21: The U.S. Navy launches the first nuclear-powered submarine, the USS *Nautilus*.

April 26:. The Geneva Conference on Korea and Indochina begins.

May 7: The French surrender to Vietminh General Vo Nguyen Giap at Dien Bien Phu in Vietnam.

September 8: The Southeast Asian Treaty Organization (SEATO) is formed, with the United States as a member.

1955

January 1: The United States begins to supply direct financial aid to South Vietnam, Cambodia, and Laos.

May 9: West Germany is admitted to full membership in the North Atlantic Treaty Organization (NATO).

1956

October 23: Hungarian revolt against Communist government and Soviet domination begins in Budapest.

October 29: War breaks out in the Middle East between Egypt and a British-French-Israeli coalition.

1957

January 5: Eisenhower enunciates the Eisenhower Doctrine.

August: The Soviets fire the first intercontinental ballistic missile.

October 4: The Soviet Union successfully launches *Sputnik*, the first artificial satellite.

1958

July–October: U.S. forces intervene in Lebanon.

October 7: The United States initiates Project Mercury, its first program for human space flight.

December 14: The United States, Britain, and France formally reject Soviet demands for their withdrawal from West Berlin.

1959

January 1: Fidel Castro assumes power in Cuba.

September 15: Soviet Premier Nikita Khrushchev arrives in the United States on a goodwill visit.

October 12: The United States places an embargo on most exports to Cuba.

1960

March 17: Eisenhower formally approves a CIA plan to train Cuban exiles for an invasion of that island.

May 1: A U-2 spy plane and its pilot, Francis Gary Powers, are shot down over the Soviet Union.

November 8: John Fitzgerald Kennedy defeats Richard Milhous Nixon in the U.S. presidential election.

1961

January 3: The United States breaks diplomatic relations with Cuba.

January 20: Kennedy is sworn in as the thirty-fifth president of the United States.

April 12: Soviet cosmonaut Yuri Gagarin becomes the first man to orbit the earth.

April 17: The Bay of Pigs invasion begins.

August 13: East Germans begin to put up the Berlin wall.

October 27: U.S. and Soviet tanks confront each other at the border between East and West Berlin.

1962

May 15: Kennedy sends five thousand U.S. Marines and fifty jet fighters to Thailand in response to Communist aggression in Laos.

July 23: Fourteen nations sign the Geneva Accords guaranteeing the neutrality of Laos.

October 14: U.S. intelligence receives photographic evidence of Soviet offensive missiles in Cuba, setting off the Cuban Missile Crisis.

1963

June 20: The United States and the Soviet Union reach the first agreement concerning the establishment of a hot line between the two nations' capitals.

July 15: The United States, Great Britain, and the Soviet Union open disarmament talks in Moscow.

November 1: A coup in South Vietnam leads to the murder of Ngo Dinh Diem, the country's president.

November 22: Kennedy is assassinated in Dallas, Texas; Lyndon Baines Johnson is sworn in as thirty-sixth president of the United States hours after the assassination.

1964

August 7: Congress passes the Gulf of Tonkin Resolution, paving the way for greater American involvement in Vietnam.

November 3: Johnson wins election, defeating Republican Barry M. Goldwater.

1965

March 2: The United States begins Operation Rolling Thunder, the sustained bombing of North Vietnam.

March 8–9: The first American combat troops, two battalions of U.S. Marines, wade ashore at Da Nang, South Vietnam.

1966

February 6–8: Johnson announces that the United States will place renewed emphasis on the effort to provide the Vietnamese people with security and new social and economic programs.

June 29: Johnson orders the bombing of oil installations at Haiphong and Hanoi, North Vietnam.

1967

June 5: War breaks out between Israel and Egypt, Jordan, and Syria.

October 21: An estimated fifty-five thousand people participate in a march on the Pentagon to protest U.S. policy in Vietnam.

1968

January 30: The Tet Offensive begins in Vietnam.

March 31: Johnson announces a halt to the bombing across ninety percent of North Vietnam and that he will not seek reelection.

April 4: Martin Luther King, Jr., is assassinated in Memphis, Tennessee.

May 12: The United States and North Vietnam open formal peace talks in Paris.

August 21: Soviet troops and tanks enter Czechoslovakia.

November 5: Richard Nixon wins the presidential election, beating Hubert H. Humphrey.

1969

January 20: Nixon is sworn in as thirty-seventh president of the United States.

March 14: Nixon decides to proceed with an anti-ballistic missile defense plan.

June 8: Nixon announces the withdrawal of twenty-five thousand troops from Vietnam.

November 17: Preliminary Strategic Arms Limitation Talks (SALT) between the United States and USSR are opened in Helsinki, Finland.

1970

April 30: Nixon announces that U.S. troops have invaded Cambodia, setting off a storm of protest across the United States.

1971

April 14: Nixon relaxes a twenty-year trade embargo against Communist China.

August 2: The United States ends twenty years of opposition to Communist China's presence in the United Nations by announcing future support of China's membership.

October 20: Henry Kissinger arrives in Beijing to arrange the agenda for the president's forthcoming trip to China.

1972

February 21: Nixon arrives in China.

May 26: President Nixon and Soviet general secretary Leonid Brezhnev sign agreements limiting both offensive and defensive nuclear weapons.

July 8: Nixon announces the sale of more than $750 million worth of wheat and other grains to the Soviet Union.

October 8: The United States and the Soviet Union sign a three-year trade agreement.

November 7: Richard Nixon is reelected president of the United States.

1973

January 23: The United States and North Vietnam sign a cease-fire accord in Paris.

June 27–July 3: Nixon and Brezhnev hold summit meetings in Moscow.

August 9: Nixon resigns the presidency; Gerald R. Ford becomes the thirty-eighth president of the United States.

1975

July 17: Spacecraft from the United States and the Soviet Union link in space.

July 30: Leaders of thirty-five nations meet in Helsinki, Finland, for the largest summit conference in European history.

1976

November 2: Democrat James Earl Carter is elected the thirty-ninth president of the United States.

1979

January 1: Formal diplomatic relations open between the United States and the People's Republic of China.

June 18: Presidents Carter and Brezhnev sign the Strategic Arms Limitation (SALT) Treaty in Vienna, Austria.

1980

November 4: Ronald Wilson Reagan is elected fortieth president of the United States, defeating Jimmy Carter.

1983

March 10: Reagan requests an increase of $110 million in military aid for El Salvador.

October 23: More than 230 U.S. Marines are killed when a truck loaded with explosives crashes into their barracks in Beirut, Lebanon.

October 25: Reagan announces that U.S. forces have invaded the Caribbean-island nation of Grenada.

November 23: American cruise missiles are deployed for the first time, in West Germany and the United Kingdom.

1984

May 24: U.S. House of Representatives passes the Boland Amendment, prohibiting further aid to the Nicaraguan Contras.

November 6: Reagan defeats Democrat Walter Mondale and is reelected president.

1985

March: Mikhail Gorbachev becomes secretary general of the Communist Party of the Soviet Union and thus the principal leader of the Soviet Union.

November 18–21: Reagan and Gorbachev hold their first summit, in Geneva.

1987

December 8: Gorbachev and Reagan sign the Intermediate-Range Nuclear Forces Treaty (INF), the first agreement in history that calls for the destruction of existing nuclear weapons.

1988

November 8: George H. Bush is elected the forty-first president of the United States, defeating Democrat Michael Dukakis.

1989

February 15: The last Soviet troops leave Afghanistan.

March 26: The first free elections in the history of the Soviet Union are held.

May 2: Hungary begins taking down the 150-mile-long fence along the Austrian border, thus opening the West to the people of the Communist bloc.

November 9: The Berlin Wall is torn down by East and West Germans.

1990

January 28: The Polish Communist Party votes to disband.

November 18–21: The Conference on Security and Cooperation in Europe puts a formal end to the cold war and places limits on both Warsaw Pact and NATO conventional forces.

1991

June 28: COMECON (Council for Mutual Economic Assistance), the Communist trade alliance, formally disbands.

July 1: The Warsaw Pact formally disbands.

August 19: Unsuccessful coup launched by hard-liners in the Soviet Union against Mikhail Gorbachev.

December 25: The Soviet Union officially disbands; Gorbachev turns over power to Boris Yeltsin in the Kremlin.

FURTHER READING

Anyone writing a survey history of the cold war must rely heavily on the vast body of written work by scholars, journalists, and diplomats on various aspects of this complicated subject. I owe this large and growing community of people a great debt. In preparing *Cold War,* I found a handful of books absolutely indispensable. John Spanier's *American Foreign Policy Since World War II* (Washington, D.C.: Congressional Quarterly Press, 1991) illuminates America's relationship to the world as a whole with precision and admirable clarity. Spanier's assessments of cold war policies and the motives behind them are evenhanded and insightful. Stephen E. Ambrose's sixth revised edition of *Rise to Globalism* (New York: Penguin, 1991) offers readers a concise, thought-provoking survey—although no leftist, Ambrose is sharply critical of American decision making—and it is a joy to read as well. The fifth edition of Walter LaFeber's *America, Russia and the Cold War* (New York: Knopf, 1985) offers a challenging interpretation of superpower relations and is particularly useful in sorting out the welter of issues and concerns of the early cold war period. LaFeber's book also contains an excellent bibliography that is worthy of close study. *Cold War, Cold Peace,* by Bernard Weisberger (New York: American Heritage, 1985), is a wise and gracefully written survey that was enormously helpful in both the writing and the research of this book. *The Cold War: Fifty Years of Conflict* (New York: Times Books, 1991), by William G. Hyland, puts forward a brilliant analysis of U.S.–USSR relations, but the reader without a solid grasp of recent history might find it tough going. Hyland is particularly good in tracing the twists and turns in Soviet and American thinking about the cold war and about each other. Readers looking for profiles of U.S. foreign-policy makers through the Ford administration should consult a reference book entitled *America's Foreign Policy 1945–1976: Its Creators and Critics* (New York: Facts On File, 1980).

For researchers seeking primary sources, see the *Guide to American Foreign Relations Since 1700,* edited by Richard Dean Burns (1983). Primary documents of the foreign policy of the United States are found in the Department of State's *Foreign Relations of the United States.*

Other books consulted that cover important issues and topics in the history of the cold war are the following:

Barson, Michael. *"Better Dead than Red!": A Nostalgic Look at the Golden Years of Russiaphobia, Red-baiting, and Other Commie Madness.* New York: Hyperion, 1992.

Bundy, McGeorge. *Danger and Survival.* New York: Random House, 1990.

Cline, Ray S. *Secrets, Spies and Scholars.* Washington, D.C.: Special Learning Corporation, 1986.

Divine, Robert A. *Politics and Diplomacy in Recent American History.* New York: Knopf, 1985.

Gaddis, John Lewis. *Strategies of Containment: A Critical Appraisal of Postwar American National Security Policy.* New York: Oxford University Press, 1982.

Halle, Louis J. *The Cold War as History.* New York: Harper & Row, 1967.

Hartmann, Frederick H. *The New Age of American Foreign Policy.* London: Macmillan, 1970.

Hodgson, Godfrey. *In Our Time: America from World War II to Nixon.* London: Macmillan, 1976.

Kennan, George F. *The Nuclear Delusion: Soviet-American Relations in the Atomic Age.* New York: Pantheon, 1983.

Knutson, April Ane, ed. *Ideology and Independence in the Americas.* Minneapolis: University of Minnesota Press, 1989.

Larson, Thomas B. *Soviet-American Rivalry.* New York: Norton, 1978.

Ranelagh, John. *The Agency: The Rise and Decline of the CIA.* New York: Simon & Schuster, 1987.

Ulam, Adam B. *The Rivals: America and Russia Since World War II.* New York: Viking, 1971.

Williams, William Appleman. *The Tragedy of American Diplomacy.* Rev. 2d ed. New York: Delta, 1972.

The 1945–60 Period

Acheson, Dean. *Present at the Creation.* New York: Norton, 1969.

Ambrose, Stephen E. *Eisenhower: The President*. New York: Simon & Schuster, 1984.

Blair, Clay. *The Forgotten War: America in Korea 1950–1953*. New York: Anchor, 1987.

Borg, Dorothy, and Walter Heinrichs, eds. *Uncertain Years: Chinese-American Relations 1947–1950*. New York: Columbia University Press, 1980.

Conquest, Robert. *Stalin: Breaker of Nations*. New York: Viking Penguin, 1992.

Donovan, John C. *The Cold Warriors*. Boston: D.C. Heath, 1974.

Fried, Richard M. *Nightmare in Red: The McCarthy Era in Perspective*. New York: Oxford University Press, 1990.

Isaacson, Walter, and Evan Thomas. *The Wise Men*. New York: Simon & Schuster, 1986.

Kennan, George F. *Memoirs 1925–1950*. Boston: Little, Brown, 1967.

—. "The Sources of Soviet Conduct." *Foreign Affairs*, July 1947, vol. 25, no. 4.

Mastny, Vojtech. *Russia's Road to the Cold War: Diplomacy, Strategy and the Politics of Communism 1941–45*. New York: Columbia University Press, 1980.

Neff, Donald. *Warriors at Suez*. New York: The Linden Press/Simon & Schuster, 1981.

Oshinski, David M. *A Conspiracy So Immense: The World of Joe McCarthy*. New York: Free Press, 1983.

Perkins, Dexter. *The Diplomacy of a New Age*. Bloomington: University of Indiana Press, 1967.

Robertson, Charles L. *International Politics since World War II: A Short History*. New York: John Wiley & Sons, 1966.

Rostow, W. W. *The Division of Europe After World War II:*

1946. Austin: University of Texas Press, 1981.

Summers, Harry G., Jr. *Korean War Almanac*. New York: Facts On File, 1990.

Taubman, William. *Stalin's American Policy*. New York: Norton, 1982.

Truman, Harry S. *Memoirs: Year of Decisions, 1945*. Garden City, N.J.: Doubleday, 1955.

Whitfield, Stephen. *The Culture of the Cold War.* Baltimore: Johns Hopkins University Press, 1991.

The 1961–80 Period

Beschloss, Michael R. *The Crisis Years: Kennedy and Khrushchev 1960–1963*. New York: HarperCollins, 1991.

Carter, Jimmy. *Keeping Faith*. New York: Bantam, 1982.

Coleman, J. D. *Incursion: From America's Chokehold on the NVA Lifelines to the Sacking of the Cambodian Sanctuaries*. New York: St. Martin's, 1991.

Fitzgerald, Frances. *Fire in the Lake: The Vietnamese and the Americans in Vietnam*. Boston: Little, Brown, 1972.

Halberstam, David. *The Best and the Brightest*. New York: Penguin, 1972.

Hyland, William G. *Mortal Rivals: Understanding the Hidden Pattern of Soviet–American Relations*. New York: Simon & Schuster, 1987.

Johnson, Haynes. *The Bay of Pigs*. New York: Norton, 1984.

Karnow, Stanley. *Vietnam: A History*. New York: Penguin, 1983.

Kearns, Doris. *Lyndon Johnson and the American Dream*. New York: Harper & Row, 1976.

Kissinger, Henry. *The White House Years.* Boston: Little, Brown, 1979.

Nixon, Richard M. *RN.* New York: Grosset & Dunlap, 1978.

Porter, Gareth, ed. *Vietnam: A History in Documents.* New York: New American Library, 1981.

Santoli, Al. *Everything We Had: An Oral History of the Vietnam War by Thirty-three American Soldiers Who Fought It.* New York: Ballantine, 1982.

Schlesinger, Arthur M., Jr. *A Thousand Days: John F. Kennedy in the White House.* Boston: Houghton Mifflin, 1965.

Sevy, Grace, ed. *The American Experience in Vietnam.* Norman: University of Oklahoma Press, 1991.

Spector, Ronald H. *After Tet: The Bloodiest Year in Vietnam.* New York: Free Press, 1993.

Summers, Harry G., Jr. *Vietnam War Almanac.* New York: Facts On File, 1985.

Ulam, Adam B. *Expansion and Coexistence: Soviet Foreign Policy 1971–1973.* New York: Praeger, 1974.

Warren, James A. *Portrait of a Tragedy: America and the Vietnam War.* New York: Lothrop, Lee & Shepard, 1990.

The 1980–91 Period

With this era we enter what is sometimes called "current history." Newspapers and magazines are a vital part of the historical record in this period, as full-length studies are few (although it should be noted that many are in the works as of this writing). In writing about this era, I found the *New York Times,* the weekly news magazine *Newsweek,* and the Facts On File *News Digest* to be quite helpful. All of these publications are usually available in medium- and large-size libraries.

Cannon, Lou. *President Reagan: The Role of a Lifetime.* New York: Simon & Schuster, 1991.

Goldman, Marshall I. *Gorbachev's Challenge.* New York: Norton, 1987.

Haig, Alexander. *Caveat.* New York: Macmillan, 1984.

Hyland, William G. *Mortal Rivals.* New York: Random House, 1987.

Kaiser, Robert G. *Why Gorbachev Happened: His Triumphs and His Failure.* New York: Simon & Schuster, 1992.

Kort, Michael. *Mikhail Gorbachev.* New York: Franklin Watts, 1990.

Kronenwelter, Michael. *The New Eastern Europe.* New York: Franklin Watts, 1991.

Lewin, Moshe. *The Gorbachev Phenomenon: A Historical Interpretation.* Berkeley: University of California Press, 1988.

Talbott, Strobe. *The Russians and Reagan.* New York: Vintage, 1984.

NOTES

1. The End . . . and the Beginning

1. Bernard Weisberger, *Cold War, Cold Peace* (New York: American Heritage, 1985), 6.
2. Quoted in Thomas B. Larson, *Soviet-American Rivalry* (New York: Norton, 1978), 4.
3. Quoted in Weisberger, *Cold War, Cold Peace,* 13.
4. Quoted in T. E. Vadney, *The World Since 1945* (New York: Facts On File, 1987), 34.
5. Quoted in Weisberger, *Cold War, Cold Peace,* 34.
6. Quoted in Weisberger, *Cold War, Cold Peace,* 54.

2. The U.S. Response: The Truman Doctrine and the Marshall Plan

1. Quoted in Alan Palmer, *The Facts On File Dictionary of World History* (New York: Facts On File, 1979), s.v. "Truman Doctrine," 370.
2. Quoted in Stephen P. Ambrose, *Rise to Globalism: American Foreign Policy Since 1938,* 6th rev. ed. (New York: Penguin Books, 1991), 82.
3. Quoted in Walter LaFeber, *America, Russia and the Cold War,* 5th ed. (New York: Knopf, 1985), 70-71.
4. George F. Kennan, "The Sources of Soviet Conduct." *Foreign Affairs,* July 1947, 575.
5. Kennan, "The Sources of Soviet Conduct," 576.

3. From the Berlin Airlift to the "Loss" of China

1. Godfrey Hodgson, *In Our Time: America from World War II to Nixon* (London: Macmillan, 1976), 118.
2. Quoted in LaFeber, *America, Russia and the Cold War,* 70.
3. Quoted in John Lewis Gaddis, *Strategies of Containment: A Critical Appraisal of Postwar American National Security Policy* (New York: Oxford University Press, 1982), 91.
4. Quoted in Gaddis, *Strategies of Containment,* 100.
5. Quoted in Ambrose, *Rise to Globalism,* 114.

4. War in Korea: 1950–53

1. Harry G. Summers, Jr., *Korean War Almanac* (New York: Facts On File, 1990), xiv.
2. Charles L. Robertson, *International Politics since World War II: A Short History* (New York: John Wiley & Sons, 1966), 140.
3. John Spanier, *American Foreign Policy since World War II,* 11th ed. (Washington, D.C.: Congressional Quarterly Press, 1991), 78.
4. Mel Elfin, "The Forgotten War," *U.S. News & World Report,* June 25, 1990, 32.

5. The Cold War at Home

1. Quoted in Richard M. Fried, *Nightmare in Red: The McCarthy Era in Perspective* (New York: Oxford University Press, 1990), 22.
2. Weisberger, *Cold War, Cold Peace,* 74–75.
3. Quoted in Fried, *Nightmare in Red,* 107.
4. Scott Siegel and Barbara Siegel, *The Encyclopedia of Hollywood* (New York: Avon, 1990), s.v. "Hollywood Ten," 203.
5. Quoted in David M. Oshinski, *A Conspiracy So Immense: The World of Joe McCarthy* (New York: Free Press, 1983), 109.
6. Quoted in Fried, *Nightmare in Red,* 123.
7. Quoted in Weisberger, *Cold War, Cold Peace,* 123.
8. Quoted in Weisberger, *Cold War, Cold Peace,* 124.
9. Stephen J. Whitfield, *The Culture of the Cold War* (Baltimore: Johns Hopkins University Press, 1991), 143.
10. Quoted in Eric Lefcowitz, "Dr. Strangelove Turns 30," *New York Times,* January 30, 1994. 24.

6. The Eisenhower Years

1. Quoted in Gaddis, *Strategies of Containment,* 154.
2. Quoted in Gaddis, *Strategies of Containment,* 128.
3. Quoted in Whitfield, *The Culture of the Cold War,* 9.
4. Quoted in Gaddis, *Strategies of Containment,* 160.
5. Quoted in Robertson, *International Politics since World War II,* 190.
6. LaFeber, *America, Russia and the Cold War,* 150.
7. Quoted in Weisberger, *Cold War, Cold Peace,* 171.
8. Quoted in Robert A. Divine, *Politics and Diplomacy in Recent American History* (New York: Knopf, 1985), 77.
9. Donald Neff, *Warriors at Suez* (New York: The Linden Press/Simon and Schuster, 1981), 25.

7. John F. Kennedy: The New Frontier and Cuba

1. Quoted in Gaddis, *Strategies of Containment,* 212.
2. Quoted in Gaddis, *Strategies of Containment,* 214.
3. G. J. A. O'Toole, *The Encyclopedia of American Intelligence and Espionage* (New York: Facts On File, 1988), s.v., "The Bay of Pigs," 49.
4. Quoted in Ambrose, *Rise to Globalism,* 146.
5. Quoted in Michael R. Beschloss, *The Crisis Years: Kennedy and Khrushchev 1960–1963* (New York: Harper Collins, 1991), 216.
6. Quoted in Beschloss, *The Crisis Years,* 223.
7. Quoted in Beschloss, *The Crisis Years,* 260.
8. Quoted in Beschloss, *The Crisis Years,* 523.
9. Quoted in Weisberger, *Cold War, Cold Peace,* 221.
10. Quoted in Beschloss, *The Crisis Years,* 541.

8. Cold War Tragedy: The War in Vietnam

1. Frances Fitzgerald, *Fire in the Lake: The Vietnamese and the Americans in Vietnam* (Boston: Little, Brown, 1972), 408.
2. Stanley Karnow, *Vietnam: A History* (New York: Viking, 1983), 250.
3. Quoted in Karnow, *Vietnam,* 323.
4. Quoted in Ronald H. Spector, *Advice and Support: The Early Years of the United States Army in Vietnam 1941–1960* (New York: Free Press, 1985), 14.
5. Weisberger, *Cold War, Cold Peace,* 235–36.
6. Quoted in Grace Sevy, ed., *The American Experience in Vietnam* (Norman: University of Oklahoma Press, 1991), 112.

7. Tim O'Brien, *Going After Cacciato* (New York: Delacorte, 1978), 61.
8. Quoted in Al Santoli, *Everything We Had: An Oral History of the Vietnam War by Thirty-three American Soldiers Who Fought It* (New York: Ballantine, 1982), 28–29.
9. Ronald Spector, *After Tet: The Bloodiest Year in Vietnam*, 8.
10. Quoted in Karnow, *Vietnam*, 514.
11. Karnow, *Vietnam*, 546.
12. Quoted in Spector, *After Tet*, 5.

9. From Nixon to Carter: 1969–80

1. Quoted in Divine, *Politics and Diplomacy in Recent American History*, 174.
2. Quoted in J. D. Coleman, *Incursion: From America's Chokehold on the NVA Lifelines to the Sacking of the Cambodian Sanctuaries* (New York: St. Martin's, 1992), 31.
3. Quoted in Weisberger, *Cold War, Cold Peace*, 264.
4. Quoted in Ambrose, *Rise to Globalism*, 244.
5. John Spanier, *American Foreign Policy Since World War II*, 206.
6. Quoted in LaFeber, *America, Russia and the Cold War*, 273.
7. Quoted in Gareth Porter, ed., *Vietnam: A History in Documents* (New York: New American Library, 1981), 438.
8. Divine, *Politics and Diplomacy in Recent American History*, 215-16.
9. Divine, *Politics and Diplomacy in Recent American History*, 220.
10. Divine, *Politics and Diplomacy in Recent American History*, 221.
11. Quoted in Ambrose, *Rise to Globalism*, 299.

10. The 1980s: Cold War II and the End of an Era

1. Lou Cannon, *President Reagan: The Role of a Lifetime* (New York: Simon and Schuster, 1991), 823.
2. Cannon, *President Reagan*, 282.
3. Quoted in William Dudley, ed., *The Vietnam War: Opposing Viewpoints*, rev. ed. (San Diego: Greenhaven Press, 1990), 183.
4. Quoted in Cannon, *President Reagan*, 314.
5. William G. Hyland, *The Cold War: Fifty Years of Conflict* (New York: Times Books, 1991), 166.
6. Quoted in Roy C. Macridis, ed., *Foreign Policy in World Politics: States and Regions* (Englewood Cliffs, NJ: Prentice-Hall, 1989), 245.
7. Quoted in Hyland, *Cold War*, 184.

8. Quoted in *Facts On File World News Digest 48,* no. 2506 (December 2, 1988), page 885.
9. Quoted in *Facts On File World News Digest 50,* no. 2609 (November 23, 1990), 861.
10. Quoted in *Facts On File World News Digest 50,* no. 2609 (November 23, 1990), 861.

11. Reflections

1. John Lewis Gaddis, *The United States and the End of the Cold War: Implications, Reconsiderations, Provocations* (New York: Oxford University Press, 1994), 13.
2. Quoted in Elaine Sciolino, "Getting in is the Easy Part of the Mission," *New York Times,* December 6, 1992, Week in Review section, 1.

FEDERAL DEFENSE BUDGET OUTLAYS 1945-91

(in millions of dollars. For fiscal year ending in year shown)

YEAR	OUTLAYS, TOTAL	NATIONAL DEFENSE
1945	92,712	82,935
1950	42,562	13,724
1955	68,444	42,729
1960	92,191	48,130
1965	118,228	50,620
1966	134,532	58,111
1967	157,464	71,417
1968	178,134	81,926
1969	183,640	82,497
1970	195,649	81,692
1971	210,172	78,872
1972	230,681	79,174
1973	245,707	78,681
1974	269,359	79,347
1975	332,332	86,509
1976	371,792	89,619
1976[1]	95,975	22,269
1977	409,218	97,241
1978	458,746	104,495
1979	504,032	116,342
1980	590,947	133,895
1981	678,249	157,513
1982	745,755	185,309
1983	808,380	209,903
1984	851,846	227,413
1985	946,391	252,748
1986	990,336	273,375
1987	1,003,911	281,999
1988	1,064,140	290,361
1989	1,143,172	303,559
1990	1,252,705	299,331
1991	1,323,441	273,292

1. Transitional quarter, July to September. Source: U.S. Office of Management and Budget, *Historical Tables, annual.*

ANNUAL NATIONAL DEFENSE SPENDING OUTLAYS AS A PERCENTAGE OF ALL GOVERNMENT SPENDING 1945-91

FISCAL YEAR	% OF FEDERAL BUDGET	% OF GROSS NATIONAL PRODUCT
1945	89.5	38.2
1946	77.3	21.1
1947	37.1	5.8
1948	30.6	3.7
1949	33.9	5.0
1950	32.2	5.1
1951	51.8	7.5
1952	68.1	13.5
1953	69.4	14.5
1954	69.5	13.3
1955	62.4	11.1
1956	60.2	10.2
1957	59.3	10.3
1958	56.8	10.4
1959	53.2	10.2
1960	52.2	9.5
1961	50.7	9.6
1962	49.0	9.4
1963	48.0	9.1
1964	46.2	8.7
1965	42.8	7.5
1966	43.2	7.8
1967	45.4	9.0
1968	46.0	9.6
1969	44.9	8.9
1970	41.8	8.3
1971	37.5	7.5
1972	34.3	6.9
1973	31.2	6.0
1974	29.5	5.6
1975	26.0	5.7
1976	24.1	5.3
1977	23.8	5.0
1978	22.8	4.8
1979	23.1	4.7
1980	22.7	5.0
1981	23.2	5.3
1982	24.9	5.9
1983	26.0	6.3
1984	26.7	6.2
1985	26.7	6.4
1986	27.6	6.5
1987	28.1	6.4
1988	27.0	6.1
1989	26.6	5.9
1990	24.8	5.4
1991	24.6	5.1

"National Defense" includes the Dept. of Defense budget and national defense functions of the Depts. of Energy and Treasury, General Services Admin., Federal Emergency Management Agency, and Selective Service. Source: *U.S. Defense and Military Fact Book.* C. W. Borklund, ABC-CLIO, 1991.

France, 18, 25, 26, 27, 29, 38, 43*n*,
   49, 54, 57, 59, 83, 115-118,
   119, 120, 122, 123, 124, 125,
   165, 175
France, occupied, 28
French Indochina War (First
   Indochina War), 83, 115-117,
   118, 152
Fuchs, Klaus, 87
Fulbright-Aiken Amendment (1973),
   196

G

Gaddis, John Lewis, 242
Geneva Conference (1954), 115,
   117, 118, 120
Geneva summit (1955), 120
Geneva summit (1985), 229
German Democratic Republic (East
   Germany), 18, 58*n*, 111-112,
   119, 143-145, 234-235, 236
German-Soviet nonaggression pact
   (1939), 26
Germany:
   division of, 18, 54-55, 117
   occupied, 29, 31-32
   postwar crises in, 54-58
   reunified, 224
Germany, Federal Republic of (West
   Germany), 54, 58, 118, 219,
   234-235
   rearming of, 54-55, 59
Germany, Nazi, 15, 20, 26-29, 30,
   43*n*, 159, 181, 247
Giap, Vo Nguyen, 168
glasnost, 19, 226-227
Gomulka, Wladislaw, 123
Gorbachev, Mikhail, 19, 208, 217*n*,
   225-233, 235-237, 240
Graebner, Norman, 141

Great Britain, 18, 25, 26, 27, 28, 29,
   43*n*, 49, 54, 57, 63, 76, 109,
   111, 112-113, 117, 119, 120,
   121, 122, 123, 124, 125, 152,
   175, 219
Greece, 39-40, 76
Greenglass, David, 87
Grenada, 215-216
Gromyko, Andrei, 192, 203, 224
Guatemala, 114-115, 245
Gulf of Tonkin Resolution (1964),
   161-162

H

Haig, Alexander M., Jr., 210-212
Haiphong, 185-186
Haiti, 216, 247
Hanoi, 185-186
Harvard University, 41, 52, 135, 136,
   181
Helman, Gerald B., 248
Helsinki Accords (1975), 199-200
Hiroshima, 59
Hiss, Alger, 84-87, 88
Hitler, Adolf, 20, 26, 27, 37, 159, 205
Ho Chi Minh, 39, 83, 116, 117, 152,
   162, 171, 242
Ho Chi Minh Trail, 160, 161, 167
Hodgson, Godfrey, 52-53
Hollywood Ten, 92
Holmes, Oliver Wendell, 85
Honduras, 114, 214
Honecker, Erich, 234
Hoover, J. Edgar, 84, 90
House of Representatives, U.S., 168,
   199
House Un-American Activities
   Committee (HUAC), 85, 91,
   92-93
Hue, 157, 170

human rights, 195, 200-201, 202, 212
Hungarian rebellion, 123-125
Hungary, 28, 43-44, 119, 123
Hussein, King of Jordan, 127
Hutchins, Robert M., 91-92
hydrogen bomb, 59, 107, 109, 187
   see also nuclear weapons

I

Inchon, 71-72
Indochina, 83, 111, 115-117, 142, 155, 196, 243
   see also French Indochina War
Indonesia, independence of, 39
intercontinental ballistic missiles (ICBMs), 126-127, 137, 145-146, 179, 192, 203, 204, 218
Internal Security Act (McCarran Act) (1950), 93-94
Iran, 33, 105, 112-113, 195, 205, 206, 215, 245
Iran hostage affair, 205, 206
Iraq, 105, 127, 204
isolationism, 9, 47, 52, 199, 248
Israel, 121, 122, 123, 197, 204, 210, 217
Italy, 25, 26

J

Japan, 26, 27, 28, 29, 31, 32, 38-39, 59, 63, 67-68
Jaruzelski, Wojciech, 220
Johnson, Lyndon B., 158-164, 170-171, 173
Jupiter missiles, 149-150
Justice Department, U.S., 84

K

Karnow, Stanley, 170
Kassem, Abdul Karim, 127
Kennan, George F., 44-46, 62-63, 65, 240
   "long telegram" of, 44
Kennedy, Jacqueline, 133
Kennedy, John F., 52, 131-153, 155, 156, 159, 163, 164, 173
Kennedy, Robert F., 141, 146
Kent State University, 184
KGB, 56, 88, 217n
Khomeini, Ayatollah Ruhollah, 204
Khrushchev, Nikita, 17, 110, 119-120, 123, 124, 125, 128-130, 134, 141-146, 148-152, 187
Kim Il-Sung, 69
Kissinger, Henry, 179, 181-185, 188-190, 192, 194-195, 197, 198, 200-201
Korea, 11, 67-80, 103
   postwar division of, 68-69
Korea, North (Democratic People's Republic of Korea), 65, 68-77, 103, 111
Korea, South (Republic of Korea), 65, 68-76, 105, 203, 221
   invasion of, 69-71
Korean War, 67-80, 87, 104, 117, 131, 163, 188
Kubrick, Stanley, 100

L

Lafeber, Walter, 111
Laos, 118, 142, 161, 196
Larson, Thomas, 12
Latin America, 114-115, 135, 137, 140-141, 211-212, 216, 243
Lattimore, Owen, 96
Latvia, 233

Lebanon, 127-128, 216-217
Lenin, V. I., 20-25, 228
Liberia, 248
Libya, 204
limited nuclear test-ban treaties, 152,
198
Lodge, Henry Cabot, 159

M

MacArthur, Douglas, 71-76, 79
in Korean War debate with
Truman, 75-76, 79
McCarran Act (Internal Security
Act) (1950), 93-94
McCarthy, Joseph R., 94-98, 103
McCarthyism, 80, 98
McCloy, John J., 52
MacFarlane, Robert S., 135, 137,
144, 146, 159, 163, 173
Maddox, 161
Malaya, 11, 105, 111
Malenkov, Georgy, 109, 110
Manchuria, 60
Manhattan Project, 87
Mao Zedong, 59-61, 188-189, 190,
242
Marine Corps, U.S., 72, 94, 127-128,
162, 164-165, 167, 199, 215,
216-217
Marshall, George Catlett, 40-41, 42,
97
Marshall Plan, 40-49, 56, 83
Marx, Karl, 20, 23
Marxist-Leninism, 10-11, 20-24, 46
Masaryk, Jan, 48
Mayaquëz, 198-199
Mazowiecki, Tadeuz, 233
Meet the Press, 85
Mexico, 216
Middle East, 32, 39, 40, 62, 105, 113,

120, 121-126, 127-128, 196-197,
204, 210, 217, 221
Mikoyan, Anastas, 139
military-industrial complex, 78, 131,
244
Minuteman missile program, 137
Mohammed Reza Pahlavi, shah of
Iran, 112-113, 204-205
Molotov, Vyacheslav, 31, 42-43
"Molotov Plan," 43
Mosaddeq, Mohammad, 112-113
Muir, John, 167
multiple independently targeted
reentry vehicles (MIRVs), 191,
192
Mumford, Lewis, 101
Mundt, Karl E., 86
Munich agreement (1938), 43, 43n,
70, 159
mutually assured destruction, 191

N

Nagasaki, 59
Nagy, Imre, 123
Nasser, Gamal Abdel, 120-122, 127
National Aeronautics and Space
Administration (NASA), 130
National Guard, U.S., 184
National Secuity Act (1947), 47
National Secuity Council, 214
National Security policy document
sixty-eight (NSC-68), 62-65
Navy, U.S., 33, 70, 127, 161
Netherlands, 27, 39, 49, 113
New York Times, 101
New Zealand, 119
Nicaraqua, 11, 140, 210, 211-212,
214, 216, 242
Niebuhr, Reinhold, 13
Nitze, Paul H., 62-64

Y

Yale University, 52, 136
Yalta Conference (1945), 29-30, 48,
        128, 181
Yeltsin, Boris, 232, 237
Yom Kippur War (1973), 197
Yugoslavia, 56, 120, 242, 247, 248

Z

Zhdanov, Andrey, 43-44
Zhou Enlai, 74, 189